THE WIDENING CIRCLE

THE WIDENING CIRCLE

Priesthood as God's way
of blessing the world

Graham Tomlin

First published in Great Britain in 2014

Society for Promoting Christian Knowledge
36 Causton Street
London SW1P 4ST
www.spckpublishing.co.uk

British Library Cataloguing-in-Publication Data
A catalogue record for this book is available from the British Library

ISBN 978–0–281–06902–6
eBook ISBN 978–0–281–06903–3

Typeset by Graphicraft Limited, Hong Kong
First printed in Great Britain by Ashford Colour Press
Subsequently digitally printed in Great Britain

eBook by Graphicraft Limited, Hong Kong

Produced on paper from sustainable forests

In memory of
Simon Featherstone
1958–2014
with deep gratitude for many years of friendship in faith

If we see Him alone, we do not see Him at all. If we see Him, we see with and around Him in ever-widening circles, His disciples, the people, His enemies and the countless millions who have not yet heard His name.

(Karl Barth)

Contents

————•◦•————

Preface

This book has been a long time in the making. It began when I was due to give a talk to students at St Mellitus College, who were about to be ordained, on the priestly role they were destined for. I had planned to give my usual (rather dull) talk on priestly ministry, and the night before, the germ of an idea fell into my mind that fitted the whole idea of priesthood into a wider framework. I decided to try out the idea on the group, hastily jotted down a few ideas, and the following morning launched into describing the broad outlines of this framework that was forming in my mind. The response was encouraging. They seemed to see that it made sense of their imminent priesthood, relating it to Christ, to the Church and to the whole way in which God dealt with the world. It seemed to place priesthood in a much larger context, a widening circle of blessing that was much more satisfying and richer than my previous attempts to describe what priesthood was about.

I later tried it out on a group of curates in the Anglican Diocese of London. As I stood up to speak, I took a deep breath. I could see that the group included the whole spectrum, from evangelicals to charismatics to catholics. Trying to speak on priesthood to such a group seemed risky, to say the least, as priesthood is the kind of subject that Anglicans tend to fall out on pretty quickly! There were those who had a very strong idea of the identity of the priest, but a less developed sense of the priesthood of the whole Church. There were also those who were very convinced of the priesthood of all believers, but who struggled to articulate a sense of what individual priestly ministry might be. At the end of the lecture, not everyone was convinced, but enough were. A few of the more catholic clergy said they recognized the version of priesthood I had explored, and some of the evangelicals found it made perfect sense to them as well. This raised another intriguing possibility: if we could find a way of talking about priesthood that both Catholic and Protestant parts of the Church could recognize, that would be a prize indeed. Whether I have succeeded is up to the reader to judge.

Since then, I have spoken on this theme several times, trying out the ideas in a number of forums, and am indebted to all those who helped shape my thinking. Alison Barr and the team at SPCK were very patient and helpful with counsel and direction, putting up with delays while other book projects intervened. In particular I am grateful to a number of theological friends with whom I have had conversations on the theme, especially Professor Tom Greggs, and Lincoln Harvey, who generously gave time during a period of study leave to read and comment on the book with his usual sharp, analytical and deeply theological cast of mind. My very good friend Simon Featherstone read the draft, at short notice, with his characteristic perceptiveness, critical mind and sympathetic ear. The book is much better as a result of his comments and advice. Very sadly, between reading the draft and the publication of the book, at the end of a year's battle with cancer, he died, full of faith and peace. The book is dedicated to him with deep gratitude for many years of friendship and wisdom. Students at St Mellitus College have also helped sharpen these ideas with their comments and questions, as I have explored the structure of the proposal with them. Needless to say, they will not all agree with what remains. I am responsible for any mistakes, and yet the book is stronger for their contributions.

My colleagues and friends at St Mellitus College are a huge joy to work with, and I am grateful to God for the chance to go to work with such a wonderful group of people whose company, wisdom and fellowship I enjoy a great deal. I am especially grateful to Simone Odendaal, who, as always, was a calm and encouraging source of support and help through the process of producing the book, correcting my typographical errors and offering some insightful comment along the way.

As always, my main gratitude is due to Sam and Jenny, Sian and Josh, and especially to Janet, whose kindness, love and faith are a constant reminder to me and to many others of Jesus the gentle and strong High Priest, the Pioneer and Perfecter of our faith.

Graham Tomlin

Introduction

The word 'priest' evokes a range of emotions. Within the Church some see it as representing the pinnacle of religious status or activity. Many a traditional religious family has glowed with pride at the thought that one of its number has entered the holy ranks of the Christian priesthood. For others, especially in more Protestant circles, it is a word they would want to avoid. Christian ministers can be described using a range of different words, but 'priest' is not one of them. Outside the Church, tragically, it is a word often and increasingly associated with another, more painful and predatory term: the word 'paedophile'. The reputation of the Christian priesthood has taken a battering in recent years, mainly in the Roman Catholic Church, but not confined to it. As a result, a word that, for many people, used to evoke feelings of pride and confidence now brings shivers of distrust.

Do a simple Google search, and one (perhaps surprising) theme that emerges is the sense of darkness surrounding the word. Images of sinister powers and evil forces abound, indicating a sense of mystery or menacing authoritarian rule, exemplified in Dan Brown's image of the Church in his book *The Da Vinci Code*. *Priest* is the title of a 2011 film in which a priest tracks down a group of faceless vampires who have kidnapped his niece, using a neat set of crucifixes that turn handily into deadly weapons when thrown. There is also a bleak 2007 novel entitled *Priest* in which a cleric is brutally murdered in an Irish town. This image of priests as those in touch with ominous secrets and clandestine ceremonies which invoke mysterious powers is rife in popular culture and film. Allied to the name 'Judas', it also conjures up, for many, a memory of one of the most influential

1

heavy metal bands in recent decades, with all the imagery of evil and darkness surrounding that genre. Already we can sense something of the ambivalence the modern world feels about the idea of priesthood. Yet this is only one side of images of priesthood in the modern world.

Alongside these darker connotations, many people have more benign images of priests. Father Ted in the eponymous TV series is an ambitious, scheming, but essentially harmless and even endearing character. The Vicar of Dibley is hardly scary. In more recent times, the TV series *Rev* depicts a struggling, doubting yet likeable figure, doing his best to be religious in a non-religious world. Think of the average TV vicar, and the image evoked is probably that of a bumbling, hesitant, possibly doubting official, usually hovering around the edges of most stories as conductors of weddings, funerals or family baptisms. Many people may know their local Anglican or Roman Catholic priests and, most of the time, they are viewed as decent, hard-working, even if culturally marginal, figures.

This strange juxtaposition, of sinister powers and inoffensive church officials, testifies to the ambiguity surrounding the idea of priesthood in contemporary culture. On one level, it seems to refer to a caste of religious officials presiding over a declining institution. Yet on the other hand, there is an awareness of intense spiritual power, which could be either good or evil. These two images are both significant in approaching the idea of priesthood today, because both indicate something important. The banal and routine nature of the lives of many ordinary clergy sits alongside a sense of bristling, transcendent mystery. It tells us that this concept of priesthood has a profundity that we often fail to recognize, yet which also touches on the mundane – it is a notion that spans our experiences of life from the humdrum to the numinous. Priesthood somehow combines the ordinary and the extraordinary, the very human and the very divine. We will return to this idea later, but first, we need to get our bearings on how we are to approach the study of priesthood.

Approaches to priesthood

If writing or reading a book can be compared to climbing a mountain, first we need to get our bearings and work out which route we are planning to take, so we can plot at least the first few steps and what equipment we will need.

Very often, Christian accounts of the concept of priesthood tend to start with the Old Testament. They begin with a description of how priests were viewed in ancient Israel. They might, for example, discuss the many shrines that existed across the land of Israel before the monarchy, pondering whether Israelite priesthood can properly be said to have emerged during the period of the Israelite kings or before. They might look at how the establishment of Solomon's Temple in Jerusalem affected Israelite priests. They might move on to changes to priesthood in the exilic period when the Temple was no longer available for Israelite worship. They then might go on to examine the specific functions of priesthood, which varied from juridical involvement in legal cases to sacrificial functions in sanctuaries, ensuring the Torah was adhered to, praying for the people and so on. They could then move on to discussing in what sense Christ was a priest, and then ask whether and how priesthood was understood in New Testament times – or even adapted from Old Testament concepts of priesthood – and on into the Patristic era and beyond.

This is one approach to understanding priesthood. It takes the view that to understand a phenomenon like this, it needs to be examined historically, or chronologically. This approach would take the form of a history of priesthood as a concept and office in the life and story of the Israelite and then Christian communities. However, it is not the same as a properly *theological* account of priesthood. The problem with this methodology is that it tends to establish a pattern of priesthood that acts as a kind of template into which later concepts have to fit. Subsequent ideas on the nature of priesthood then end up being forced into this as a kind of Procrustean bed that shapes the nature of, and assumptions about, priesthood from the start. It might be a valid approach historically, but is not ideal theologically.

Another approach might be the 'history of religions' approach.[1] Besides Old Testament, Israelite priests, there are of course Hindu, as well as Zoroastrian, Shinto, Wicca and Taoist priests. Given that there are priests in a number of different religions, a starting point might be to make a comparative study of priesthood as understood in different religious contexts. This methodology might look at how priests operate in such religious contexts, perhaps examining the links between priesthood and caste or heredity, the relationship between priesthood and shamanism, or the role of priests as cultic officials. It might then proceed to examine what they have in common, and draw out an understanding of priesthood from there, one that holds across religious traditions, while recognizing the differences between them. This is a valid and fascinating exercise in itself, but again, like the historical approach, is not the same as a theological understanding of priesthood.

The historical starting point for a theology of priesthood might be Old Testament priests, and a religious starting point might be the way in which it works in different sacred traditions. Theologically, however, the starting point cannot be either of these. If we are to begin a properly Christian theological account of priesthood, the starting point has to be somewhere else – it has to lie in the nature and action of God. And if one main line of Christian theology is right, from St Paul through Athanasius, to Luther and in more recent times to theologians such as Karl Barth, the starting point for all theological endeavour has to be God's presence and work in the person of Christ, God's chosen one.

Priesthood and election

Priesthood in the Bible is intimately associated with the doctrine of election. In Exodus 19, at the crucial moment of the giving of the law to Israel at Sinai, this defining moment in the history of divine encounter with Israel, the ideas of priesthood and election coincide:

> You yourselves have seen what I did to Egypt, and how I carried you on eagles' wings and brought you to myself. Now if you obey me fully and keep my covenant, then out of all nations you will be my treasured possession. Although the whole earth is mine, you will be for me a kingdom of priests and a holy nation.
>
> (Exod. 19.4–6)

The nation of Israel is chosen as a priestly kingdom out of all the nations of the earth. At this early stage of the Bible, priesthood is connected intimately with the notion that God chooses. At the same time, the author brings together the themes of creation and election. Although the whole earth belongs to God, created as a reflection of his glory and goodness, he has chosen this particular people as a 'kingdom of priests'. Out of the whole, he chooses a part.

This is a characteristic mark of divine activity throughout the Bible: this constant, sometimes embarrassing, tendency to be selective. In the book of Genesis alone, God repeatedly chooses parts out of the whole. Out of all of the animal life of the created world he chooses humanity to bear his image (1.26–27). He chooses Abel's offering rather than that of Cain (4.4–5). Out of what has become a wretched, chaotic race, he chooses Noah and his family (6.8) to be the origin of a new humanity, saved through the flood. After the flood he chooses Abraham rather than any other (12.2), Isaac not Ishmael (21.12), Jacob not Esau (ch. 25), Joseph rather than the other sons of Jacob (chs 37, 39—50), Ephraim not Manasseh (48.14) and so on. Each time there is a choice of one over another, the selection of one out of many.

Now of course this raises the question as to why God chooses, why he insists on being so discriminatory and apparently exclusive. And this is where we need to distinguish between three different aspects of this question, referring to the *purpose, grounds* and *nature* of God's choice.

With reference to the *purpose* of God's choice, we are given a reason as to why God chooses. The paradigmatic instance of this is in the choice of Abraham in Genesis 12. There, Abraham is chosen specifically so that he might be a blessing to the rest of humanity:

> I will make you into a great nation, and I will bless you; I will make your name great, and you will be a blessing. I will bless those who bless you, and whoever curses you I will curse; and all peoples on earth will be blessed through you. (Gen. 12.2–3)

Abraham is chosen out of the whole of humanity *so that he might be a blessing to the rest of his race*. The part is chosen as a means of blessing the whole. The same pattern is discernible in many of the other divine choices in the book of Genesis. Adam is chosen out of the rest of Creation so that he might 'work and take care' of the rest of the earth (2.15). Noah is chosen so that, through him, Creation might be preserved and restored (6.20). Election is never for privilege but always for blessing. Those chosen are selected to be the divine means of bringing blessing to the whole of which they are a part.[2]

In another sense, however, with regard to the *grounds* for God's choice, no straightforward answer is given. When we ask why this one rather than that, we are deliberately not given a reason as to why God chooses. A classic example is the story of Cain and Abel. Abel's offering was acceptable before God whereas Cain's was not. Why? We are not told.

Commentators have tried to come up with various reasons why Abel's offering was better than Cain's, but in the end, the text doesn't tell us in any obvious way.[3] The closest the Old Testament comes to an answer to the mystery of the grounds of God's choice is the one given in Deuteronomy 7.7–8:

> The LORD did not set his affection on you and choose you because you were more numerous than other peoples, for you were the fewest of all peoples. But it was because the LORD loved you and kept the oath he swore to your ancestors that he brought you out

with a mighty hand and redeemed you from the land of slavery, from the power of Pharaoh king of Egypt.

This is both an answer and not an answer. It gives the negative – reasons which do not count – yet when it comes to the positive attribution of motives for God's choice it simply says that this choice is grounded in the divine love and faithfulness. In other words, the grounds of God's choice are found not in any characteristic or feature of the object of his choice (in Israel's size, holiness or potential, or in Cain or Abel's prior goodness or evil) but in his own will and character. This, of course, does not get us any further with regard to the question of why God chooses one as opposed to another. It is simply hidden in the mystery of the divine will, choice or election.

Now this idea has given rise in theological history to the notion of the hiddenness of God's will, the 'divine decree'. When John Calvin discusses the question of election and why some are chosen over others, he resorts to this idea of a secret divine decision: 'we must always at last return to the sole decision of God's will, the cause of which is hidden in him . . . No other cause of this fact can be adduced but reprobation, which is hidden in God's secret plan.'[4]

Karl Barth, in one of his major contributions to twentieth-century theology, questioned Calvin over this very point. In an extended discussion of the doctrine of election in II.2 of *Church Dogmatics*, Barth critiques any doctrine of predestination or election that is not Christologically conditioned and rooted. For Barth, outside of Christ, there is no election. Election is based in sheer grace: 'God elects. It is this that precedes absolutely all other being and happening.'[5] And more to the point, 'God's eternal will is the election of Jesus Christ.'[6] There is no *decretum absolutum* before the choice of God to be his own Word, Jesus Christ. God has chosen, in the beginning, to be gracious towards humankind in Jesus Christ, so that 'divine predestination is the election of Jesus Christ'.[7]

Barth's doctrine of election as God's decision to be gracious towards humankind in Jesus Christ gives content to this discussion of the grounds of God's choice. In other words, it is a clue to the third aspect of this question: the *nature* of that choice. God's primary object of choice is neither humanity, nor Israel, nor Christians, nor the elect, nor you or me, but Christ. The word 'Christ' of course, comes from '*Christos*', the Greek version of 'messiah', the 'anointed', or 'chosen one'. According to Barth, this choice reveals to us the ultimate will of God, and because this very Christ is both God and man, divine and human, it indicates the eternal will of God to be 'for us', in the conjunction of humanity and divinity in him. Barth points out that only if God's election is tied firmly to his eternal choice of Christ, rather than some mysterious 'eternal decree' whereby he chooses to save some and damn others (as is suggested by both Augustine and Calvin), can the divine choice be an occasion for joy, rather than anxiety or fear. If election concerns a secret decree, mysteriously made in the hidden depths of the unknown divine will, then the result is an anxious wondering whether you are one of the elect or not: that characteristic worry of the Protestant Reformed Christian that Barth knew so well. If God has chosen Christ, and therefore has chosen humanity in Christ, then his ultimate word towards us is not 'no' or even 'maybe', but 'yes'. Christ, the chosen one of God, gives shape and content to the will of God, as he heals, teaches and gives life to those he encounters – this is what the will of God looks like. The life of Christ is a divine affirmation of humanity, rather than a hidden mysterious blank.[8] It is the reason for Christian freedom and joy – and it is all based on election.

Now where does this emphasis on election take us? It tells us where to begin our explorations. If God chooses a part of the whole in order to be the means of his blessing the whole, and if this is somehow central to what priesthood means, then this points directly at Jesus Christ, God's chosen one. If Christ is the true chosen one of God, the one through whom God blesses the world, this means that he is the true priest, the one from whom all priesthood takes its shape and meaning. We must begin not with history, nor with *Religionsgeschichte* – the historical study of religion – but with Christ. To understand what priesthood means, we start with Jesus.

This focus on the priesthood of Christ as the starting point and central theme of our explorations, as it happens, takes us back to our original thoughts on the strange way in which the idea of priesthood combines the numinous and the ordinary, the sense of powerful mysterious forces, and familiar, mundane reality. If Christ is the true priest, then this somehow makes sense of this blend of the ordinary and the extraordinary. As we shall explore in the next few chapters, Christ the Son of God is the incarnate Word, the one in whom ordinary humanity and divine presence come together. As the true High Priest, he feels weariness, hunger and pain; yet he also walks on water and raises the dead. In him we see both strands of priestly reality, the mundane and the heavenly, the routine and the remarkable, the normal and the numinous.

Jesus the priest

The notion of Jesus as a priest is in fact more of a story than an idea. When we look at the way in which the New Testament speaks of the priesthood of Christ, it takes a trajectory, a narrative shape that builds up a picture of what his priesthood consists of and what it accomplishes.

The main text in which the New Testament develops a theology of priesthood is, of course, the letter to the Hebrews, which consists, at least in part, of an extended reflection on the application of the idea of priesthood (*hiērōsunē*) to Christ. What does the priesthood of Christ consist of? What does it mean to call him the true High Priest? Or in other words, what is there about Christ that makes him a priest? We will look in more detail at the letter to the Hebrews in the next couple of chapters, but first, a little orientation.

The letter to the Hebrews begins in a startlingly direct way. Unlike any other New Testament epistle, there is no greeting, no prolegomena. It gets straight to the point: God has now spoken to us by a Son. This 'Son' of God (1.2) is the heir of all things, an exact reflection of the divine glory, bearing the very imprint of the divine nature, through whom God has created and sustained the world. After arguing for the superiority of the Son to angels, the idea of the priesthood of Christ is introduced in a dense and significant statement:

> For this reason he had to be made like them, fully human in every way, in order that he might become a merciful and faithful high priest in service to God, and that he might make atonement for the sins of the people. (2.17)

This immediately connects Christ's identity as priest with two major Christian doctrines: incarnation and atonement. This Jesus (1.9, 11) became 'a merciful and faithful high priest' in the movement of both incarnation ('made like them, fully human in every way') and atonement ('that he might make atonement for the sins of the people'). The first mark of the priesthood of Christ is therefore this downward movement, of becoming human in the incarnation and enduring death on a cross.

In the incarnation, Christ reveals God to us. His body is the location of God's presence in the world, and thus he mediates God to us, revealing his nature and being in human form. Christ is the image of the invisible God, 'the radiance of God's glory and the exact representation of his being' (Heb. 1.3). In the incarnation, God makes himself available to us, and accommodates himself to human form, as Calvin would put it.[9] God is mediated to us in the person of Christ. Furthermore, as this text reminds us, the priesthood of Christ connects with the doctrine of the atonement. Christ is both priest and victim – offering a sacrifice for sins, just as priests do in the Temple day after day.

In the last stage of the story, the idea of priesthood is connected to a further vital Christian doctrine, the ascension:

> Therefore, since we have a great high priest who has ascended
> into heaven, Jesus the Son of God, let us hold firmly to the faith
> we profess. For we do not have a high priest who is unable to
> empathize with our weaknesses, but we have one who has been
> tempted in every way, just as we are – yet he did not sin. Let us
> then approach God's throne of grace with confidence, so that we
> may receive mercy and find grace to help us in our time of need.
>
> (Heb. 4.14–16)

After the downward movement of incarnation to atonement – in
which Christ brings God near to humankind, in which he unites
humanity to himself – in the resurrection and ascension, there is
a corresponding upward movement, whereby Christ brings us
back to God. Christ's ascension leads to the idea of his mediatory
intercession for us:

> Because Jesus lives for ever, he has a permanent priesthood. There-
> fore he is able to save completely those who come to God through
> him, because he always lives to intercede for them.
>
> (Heb. 7.24–25)

The priesthood of Christ in Hebrews therefore is a story, a narrative, a journey that follows a distinct path. It starts with the road
downwards in incarnation and atonement, the road that leads
from the right hand of the exalted Father in the courts of heaven
to the right hand of an executed criminal outside the walls of
Jerusalem. It then takes a new trajectory – the road upwards
through resurrection and ascension, back to that very right hand
of the Father, bringing humanity with him, now able to intercede
for that very human race of which he became a part.

If our starting point on the mountain is with the priesthood
of Christ, the next couple of chapters will begin to spell out what
this means in charting the trajectory of that priesthood in these
two movements of the story of Jesus the priest – the 'downward'
movement of incarnation and atonement, and an 'upward' one in
resurrection and ascension. From that point onwards, we begin
to sketch out how this priesthood is played out within the world:

11

first in humanity itself, called to play a priestly role between God and Creation; then in the Church, which also acts as a priestly mediator between God and the rest of humanity; and then finally in the person of the minister him- or herself, who also acts in a priestly manner towards the rest of the Church. In each case, the part is called to be the means by which the whole becomes all that it was intended to be, in an ever-widening circle of divine blessing.

1

The priesthood of Christ: descent

As soon as you start reading the letter to the Hebrews, you find yourself breathing the air and surveying the landscape of first-century Judaism, with its priests, the bloody and messy sacrifices in the Temple in Jerusalem, and its Old Testament fund of memory. Today, most of its readers don't have this kind of background, which means that the letter to the Hebrews can seem rather arcane, a quite alien text. So when the author of Hebrews identifies 'Jesus the Son of God' as the 'great high priest' (4.14), this bold statement identifying Jesus in this priestly role, superseding all other priesthood, can seem remote, strange, not meaning a great deal. Yet there may be something deeply hidden within this idea of Jesus the priest that sheds light on a whole range of issues that affect us in the modern world. To get there, however, we will need to do quite a bit of work to uncover the contours of this idea and how it plays out in the rest of the Bible, and indeed how it shapes a whole new understanding of the world and our place in it.

The original Christian readers of this text understood the world out of which the letter grew.[1] It was the institution of the high priesthood in the Jerusalem Temple, a priesthood that followed the Old Testament pattern of being descended from the line of Aaron.[2] Jesus is called a priest, just like those Temple priests. However, the author makes a crucial distinction: Christ is a priest not of the order of Aaron, as the Temple priests were, but of an earlier, more basic and original priesthood – that of Melchizedek.

This refers back to the story in Genesis 14 where Melchizedek blesses Abraham:

> Then Melchizedek king of Salem brought out bread and wine.
> He was priest of God Most High, and he blessed Abram, saying,
> 'Blessed be Abram by God Most High, Creator of heaven and earth.
> And praise be to God Most High, who delivered your enemies into
> your hand.' (Gen. 14.18–20)

The more specific idea followed up in Hebrews, however, is the
further reference to this story in Psalm 110, a Davidic psalm which
applies the Melchizedek priesthood to the house of David: 'The
LORD has sworn and will not change his mind: "You are a priest
for ever, in the order of Melchizedek"' (Ps. 110.4).

David, of course, was a king, not a priest. He was not a member
of the house of Aaron, so that this designation of David as both
priest and king was somewhat controversial. It extended the office
of priesthood both beyond the bounds of the tribe of Aaron and,
indeed, before it. It raised the idea of an original priesthood –
a kind of primeval priesthood that existed before and beyond
the Aaronic Temple priesthood of Israel. Christ's priesthood was
no ordinary priesthood – it was modelled not on Aaron's but on
another and earlier type altogether.

Now this might seem like an attempt to argue for the precedence
of Christ's priesthood over the Jewish one, by simply referring to
an older model. When we look closer, however, the letter to the
Hebrews goes beyond even this. It is not just that the priesthood
of Melchizedek is chronologically older than the Aaronic priesthood. The priesthood of Melchizedek is actually timeless, located
outside history: 'Without father or mother, without genealogy,
without beginning of days or end of life, resembling the Son
of God, he remains a priest for ever' (Heb. 7.3). This text, in fact,
reverses the expected order of priestly origins. It is not so much
that Christ's priesthood is modelled on Melchizedek's but it is
the other way round. Melchizedek 'resembl[es] the Son of God',
rather than *vice versa*. We find ourselves taken further back in
time and even before time. The priesthood of Christ is before
the Jerusalem Temple priests, before David, before Aaron, before
Melchizedek even – it is the priesthood of the Son of God.

Melchizedek's priesthood is a model of an even more primal form of priesthood than that seen in the Old Testament story of the meeting of Abraham with this mysterious priest of Salem. This is an eternal priesthood, located not so much in time but in eternity, in the realm of God, not human history. Hebrews argues therefore that the priesthood of Christ comes before any historical priestly model, whether that of Aaron or any other form of priesthood.

Christ is a 'priest' in a way that is like, but at the same time unlike, the familiar priests of the Jerusalem Temple. His priesthood is more elemental, something built into the very fabric of being, even before the very beginning of all things. This is borne out by another theme brought out by the author of Hebrews: the role of Christ in Creation.

Christ the clue to Creation

As Hebrews says, it was through this very 'Son of God', the one that is also the true and ultimate High Priest (4.14), that Creation came into being:

> in these last days he has spoken to us by his Son, whom he appointed heir of all things, and through whom also he made the universe. The Son is the radiance of God's glory and the exact representation of his being, sustaining all things by his powerful word.   (1.2–3)

Creation is the work of God, performed through the Son. Creation comes into being and is shaped by the nature of the Son, who is the exact representation of God's very nature. In fact, there is more: the whole Creation not only came into being through the Word, but is also preserved moment by moment by that same Word who 'sustain[s] all things'.

In other words, God mediates himself to the world through the Son. The world comes into being through the pre-existent Son, and is entirely dependent on him.[3] This basic idea is of course found elsewhere in the New Testament, in different language.

A similar idea occurs in John's Gospel where God creates the world through the '*Logos*', or Word (John 1.3). John adopts the contemporary Stoic idea of the pre-existent principle of Reason, '*Logos*', to convey the relationship between God and Creation through Christ.[4] The first chapter of Colossians is the other classic passage that expounds this idea:

> The Son is the image of the invisible God, the firstborn over all creation. For in him all things were created: things in heaven and on earth, visible and invisible, whether thrones or powers or rulers or authorities; all things have been created through him and for him. He is before all things, and in him all things hold together.
>
> (Col. 1.15–17)

The Son reveals God as 'the image of the invisible God, the firstborn over all creation' (v. 15). He also reveals the true nature of Creation: 'in him all things were created: things in heaven and on earth, visible and invisible, whether thrones or powers or rulers or authorities; all things have been created through him and for him' (v. 16). The true nature of Creation is thus revealed as being oriented and related to Christ. The Son bears the very stamp of God's nature, and in turn, Creation bears the imprint of the nature of the Son. He is the *prototokos* (Col. 1.15, 18), the firstborn or 'prototype' as it were, of both Creation (v. 15) and new Creation (v. 18) so that Creation is no longer just an object explicable on its own, but something that finds its true meaning and identity as related to Christ. Creation is Christ-shaped, or at least it was in its original intention, and will be when finally brought to completion.[5]

The Son therefore acts as a Mediator between God and Creation, the one through whom the world came into being, the one whose being and character shapes the very nature of the world, and who in turn sustains it moment by moment until its fulfilment.

Hebrews also suggests another way in which the Son acts as Mediator: between God and humanity. He is said to be 'the radiance of God's glory and the exact representation of his being'

(1.3), yet he also 'feel[s] sympathy for our weaknesses' (4.15) and enters into the 'inner sanctuary' of the heavenly realms 'on our behalf' (6.20). This same idea of Christ as Mediator between God and humanity is found elsewhere in the New Testament: 'For there is one God and one mediator between God and mankind, the man Christ Jesus, who gave himself as a ransom for all people' (1 Tim. 2.5–6). The Son stands between God and Creation, yet he also stands more specifically between God and humanity as Mediator. Karl Barth writes: 'Between God and man there stands the person of Jesus Christ, Himself God and Himself Man, and so mediating between the two. In Him, God reveals Himself to man. In Him man sees and knows God.'[6] This dense statement makes a bold claim, that in Jesus Christ it is possible to see both humanity and God, yet it also raises the question of what we mean when we say that Christ stands between God and humanity, mediating between them.

Intermediary or mediator?

All mediation involves the mediator identifying in some way with both parties. Negotiators who try to settle disputes need to have some sympathy with both sides, some understanding of what it is like to be on one side or the other of the debate, otherwise they cannot bring any effective reconciliation.

So what kind of Mediator is Jesus Christ? And how exactly does the Son relate to the 'parties' he mediates between: God and the world, or God and humanity? Fundamental to Jewish and therefore early Christian thought was the distinction between God and Creation. God is the Creator of the world, not part of it. The world is not God, God is. Whereas a good deal of ancient paganism was effectively a kind of nature worship, blurring the distinctions between God and Creation, both Judaism and early Christianity avoided that idea like the plague, insisting on a strict demarcation between God and Creation. Yet once a radical distinction is drawn between God and the world, the question arises of how the world comes into being, and what is the relationship between God and the world; hence the emergence of the idea of mediation.

Now this idea of 'mediation' between God and the created order has something of a chequered history in Christian theology. Much of that history stems from a set of beliefs about the world at the time in which early Christianity was emerging. One aspect of the general first-century world view was a sense of God's distance from the world, in some ways similar to the Jewish-Christian distinction between God and Creation, but in other ways quite different from it. Whereas Judaism and the early Christians held to the radical difference between God and Creation, while at the same time asserting the goodness of the created order, many Greek pagan thinkers modified that sense of difference, because they observed that Creation was not necessarily all good, and God cannot be responsible for what is less than good. They therefore wanted to distance God from the world, not because it was the free Creation of a good God, but because a good God cannot have created such a flawed world.

Another key set of ideas (although there were various versions of this) was that of a hierarchy of being, a kind of gradation of existence, with God at the top, inanimate objects at the bottom and all kinds of other forms of life – humans, animals, angels, etc. – in between. This was a way in Greek thinking of maintaining the distance or separation between God and Creation, yet establishing some continuity between them.

One of the central ideas of Platonism, discussed in Plato's *Dialogues*, and still exercising an influence even as late as the first century and beyond, was that of the Platonic 'Forms' – a set of ideal, perfect entities that exist on a metaphysical plane above this phenomenal world, of which everything physical is but an imperfect copy. So, for example, every individual dog is an imperfect copy or instance of the universal 'Idea' or 'Form' of 'Dog'. The way we are able to identify a particular thing as a dog, similar to other dogs, is the relation of this individual instance of a dog – despite it being of a different breed, size, shape, etc. from other dogs – to the Idea or Form of 'Dog', something in which all individual dogs share. These Forms are immaterial, yet, Plato insists, more real than the physical world, as he thought spiritual reality to be more, not less, real than the physical world. God or 'the Good' created this world, therefore, according to the pattern of these Forms. They therefore act as a kind of mediating level between God and the created order, allowing a certain divine distance from the messy business of physicality.

A system of thought that particularly challenged early Christian theology along somewhat similar lines in the second century was the strange mixture of philosophies or mythologies that are grouped under the name of 'Gnosticism'. There are many types of Gnosticism, but generally speaking, it was a dualistic cast of thought, assuming a radical divide between the divine and the created.[7] In Valentinian Gnosticism for example, the Father begets the *Pleroma* or 'Fullness'. This consists of other divine beings, with various grades of divinity, often known as *Aeons*, with one of these, the *Demiourgos*, identified as the Creator God. This figure is necessarily distinct from the *Pleroma*, as the latter cannot by definition have anything to do with physical matter. This *Demiourgos* thus created the world, acquitting the *Pleroma* or the Father of any responsibility for its fallibility and imperfection. The *Demiourgos* also emits *Archons*, yet further semi-divine beings who act as intermediaries between God and Creation. The *Pleroma* also brings forth the Holy Spirit and Christ, who comes to earth in a kind of spiritual body which redeems the spirit and not the flesh. This set of ideas is very different from that of the Platonic Forms, yet shares with it a cosmology which assumes a number of intervening entities, or mediators, if you like, between God and Creation.

Both of these were soon discarded as not authentically Christian options;[8] and yet this basic idea, that there needs to be some kind of mediator between God and Creation, resurfaces in one of the early Christological heresies, rejected in the fifth-century Council of Chalcedon, namely the ideas associated with the Eutychian heresy.[9]

Eutyches was a fifth-century theologian based in Constantinople. He reacted strongly to the teaching of Nestorius, who, twenty or so years earlier, had wanted to distinguish sharply the human and divine natures of Christ, thus arguing that Christ was made up of two quite distinct natures, one human and the other divine. Believing that this approach separated divinity from humanity too radically, Eutyches proposed the opposite idea, that Christ possessed only one nature after the union of the human and divine in the incarnation – a new, single nature of the incarnate Word. Eutyches was attempting to be loyal to the teaching of the great Cyril of Alexandria, Nestorius' great nemesis, who had argued passionately for the essential unity of the divine and human in Christ; however, Eutyches lacked Cyril's fine grasp of distinctions. He ended up with a clumsy attempt to resolve these early Christological debates in which the proper humanity of Christ was no longer fully intact. For Eutyches, the Word actually 'became flesh' (rather than 'assuming flesh'). In other words, the Word of God 'turned into' flesh, resulting in a being that was neither fully divine, yet neither was he really human in any proper sense of the word. Any distinction between the divine and human in Christ was therefore entirely erased.

At the Council of Chalcedon in AD 451, the teachings of both Nestorius and Eutyches were condemned as the two extreme poles of a spectrum of Christological views. Eutyches' account of the person of Christ would have had the benefit of simplicity, but would have suggested a Son who was neither properly divine nor human. In other words, Eutyches' Christ was a *tertium quid*, a 'third thing', neither properly divine nor fully human, yet seeking to act as an intermediary between them. Eutychianism is very different from Platonism or Gnosticism, yet it too shares the same tendency to posit a mediating being between God and the world that belongs, strictly speaking, to neither. In his attempt to unite divinity and humanity in Christ, Eutyches ended up dividing them – they can only be linked by a third entity, the Son who is neither properly human, nor properly divine.

The various attempts to solve the problem of the relationship of God to the world in Platonism, Gnosticism and Eutychianism all make the same mistake: they propose the need for an inter-mediary, rather than a mediator between God and the world. In other words, they suggest the need for a kind of arbitrator, a go-between, who can link the divine and the created. In the case of both Platonism and Gnosticism, this is because there is a fundamental incompatibility between God and Creation. Creation has to be the product of the Forms, or the *Demiourgos*, rather than the Father himself, because ultimate divinity cannot have anything to do with physical matter, imperfect and tainted as it is in its very being. Between God and Creation there needs to be a third entity, connecting them together.

The early Christian struggle to articulate a proper Christology, an understanding of the person of Christ that was true both to the historical memory of the person of Jesus of Nazareth and to the Old Testament witness to the nature of God, could never settle for any of these ideas. This was not least because of the fundamental conviction of the goodness of Creation. If God made the world, without the help of any intermediary beings, and that Creation was at the beginning thoroughly 'good' (Gen. 1.31), then there was no need for a radical distance between God and physical matter. There was a desire to maintain the very important distinction between the divine and the created (early Christianity could not venture down the path of pagan nature worship, as if the world itself was divine) but not a distance. The result was a distinctive kind of Christology: a Christology of mediation, not intermediation.

To further explain this point, the image of a bridge might help. The Bosphorus is the narrow strip of water that divides Europe from Asia, running through the city of Istanbul (a suburb of which, incidentally, is now Kadiköy, the ancient site of the Council of Chalcedon). It is crossed by the Fatih Sultan Mehmet Bridge, which spans the strait at its narrowest point. As a bridge, it connects the two continents, but does not unite them. They still remain separate entities, so that you are either (on one side of the bridge) in Europe, or (on the other) in Asia. You cannot be in both at the same time. This is why the image of Christ as a kind of bridge between two sides of a chasm is not very helpful. A bridge between two river banks does not share the nature of the things it unites – the banks of the river. It is actually a third entity that does the work of uniting, yet only by being something different from the things that need uniting.

Platonism, Gnosticism and Eutychianism all held various versions of the 'bridge' understanding of the relationship between the divine and the human. God and Creation are so distinct, so *different*, that some kind of intermediary is needed to bring them together. There are of course many modern versions of this same idea. Seances and spiritualism of various kinds all interject various ghostly beings between us poor bodily bound humans and the world beyond. The result is the possibility of some distant relationship, or dim, misty contact between the physical world and the mysterious realm beyond, but no real knowledge of it, let alone any possibility of union with it.

Christ the Mediator

The Christology that emerged from the long, intricate and sometimes furious debates over the understanding of the person of Christ was quite different from this, for good reasons. The Son of God, through whom the world came into being, the one Mediator between God and humanity *shared the nature of both.* The early Fathers struggled to find positive images to convey this idea. A common one was of an iron rod thrust into a fire until it burns red hot. The iron shares in the nature of iron, and also of fire, but is not a third separate substance from iron and fire. Perhaps the reason that they struggled was because Christ's mediation is in a sense unique, or at least unique in the extent of his identification with both humanity and divinity. Human mediators (for example, international diplomats, arbitrators in industrial disputes, divorce lawyers, etc.) need to understand and empathize with both of the parties between which they mediate. Christ's mediation goes beyond this: he not only identifies and understands, he shares the very nature of both of the parties between which he mediates: God and humanity. This is why he is truly able to unite and reconcile God and his Creation, not just bring about an uneasy truce between them. The early Christians were convinced that something unique had happened in Christ – that heaven and earth had been finally united – and their Christological debates were all about how to do justice to this profound act of mediation, or reconciliation, that had taken place.

The famous Chalcedonian definition of Christology from AD 451 states:

> We all with one voice confess our Lord Jesus Christ, one and the same Son, the same perfect in Godhead, the same perfect in Manhood, truly God and truly man ... Of one substance with the father as touching the Godhead, the same of one substance with us as touching the manhood ... *one and the same, without confusion, without change, without division, without separation, the distinction of the natures being in no way abolished because of the Union,* but rather the characteristic property of each nature being preserved and concurring into one person and one subsistence, not as if Christ were parted or divided into two persons, but one and the same Son and only-begotten God, Word, Lord Jesus Christ [emphasis added].

What this claims is that in the person of Christ we find both full divinity and full humanity. The Chalcedonian definition was keen to preserve the full humanity and the full divinity of his person. He was not 50 per cent divine and 50 per cent human as Nestorius had implied, nor was he a 100 per cent blend of divinity and humanity, as Eutyches had suggested. Full, perfect divinity was preserved in him, as was full, perfect humanity – 100 per cent human and 100 per cent divine at the same time, even if that stretches the capacities of our limited understanding.

The point of this was that if there was to be a mediator between God and Creation, or between God and humanity, who would genuinely reconcile them, and make possible an intimate transforming union between them, that mediator needed to share the full nature of both. He was not a bridge that linked them, but a person in whom they were united, a person in whom they fully overlapped, as it were. As a result, the idea of a proper, intimate unity between us and God comes within reach. Eutyches' Christology, along with the Platonic Forms and Gnostic intermediaries, would suggest that a somewhat distant, rather nodding relationship with God might be possible, a polite recognition that one might have with a distant relation, but not a close, intimate union. Only if Christ was the true Mediator, uniting humanity and divinity in his person, did the prospect of radical transformation of human life, and indeed the whole Creation, become possible.

The priesthood of Christ

If the Son is the Mediator between God and Creation, and at the same time, as the letter to the Hebrews suggests, he is the true High Priest, this begins to help us see what this priesthood means. Christ's mediating priesthood depends on his sharing in both full divinity ('the radiance of God's glory, and the exact representation of his being' – Heb. 1.3) and full humanity ('like them, fully human in every way, in order that he might become a merciful and faithful high priest in service to God' – Heb. 2.17), sharing entirely in human experience, except for the experience of sinning.[10]

The author of Hebrews emphasizes the extent to which the Son enters the human condition. Jesus is fully human. If he is not, then humanity cannot be infused with divinity, it cannot have the divine image restored to it, or, in the language of the letter to the Hebrews, he cannot 'help those who are being tempted' (2.18). Neither Nestorius nor Eutyches in their very different ways can really conceive of Christ being both human and divine at the same time; for them, humanity and divinity are two different things, like stone and water, or Asia and Europe – connected, but never really united.

The pastoral and spiritual dimensions of this are significant. The problem with a Eutychian type of Christology is that blending together humanity and divinity in one person always tends to mean that the human gets overwhelmed by the divine. Eutyches actually leads us toward the conclusion that that is what always happens when God enters a human life – humanity never survives the impact. Ultimately, Eutychian Christology dissolves humanity, devalues it, and, as a result, it disappears.[11] Nestorian Christology, which separates divinity and humanity into two entirely distinct principles within the same person, keeps us apart from God – so near, and yet so far – with no possibility of ever sharing in any way in the divine life. Christ's mediating priesthood, based in his full and entire humanity, validates and affirms humanity and gives it a significance which makes it possible to even share in that same priesthood, as we will explore later in this book. It also opens the possibility of real fellowship – *koinonia* – with God, where we can enjoy real intimacy, even participation in the life of God himself, while still preserving the distinction between the Creator and the Creation.

Christ is priest because he is the Mediator – the one who binds together both humanity and divinity in one. The incarnate Son is not a third party who reconciles humanity and God. Instead, Christ's mediation between God and humanity is dependent on his sharing the full nature of both. Christ is Mediator precisely as both human and divine. The priesthood of Christ refers not so much to his identity as the eternal Word, or even as the Son, but in particular to his unique divine–human nature. Unless Christ is 'made like them, fully human in every way', as one translation puts it, he cannot become 'a merciful and faithful high priest' (Heb. 2.17).

Christ's priesthood therefore resides in the union of his divinity and humanity. If he were solely divine he could not be the true

High Priest; neither could he be so if he were solely human.[12] He can only be the true Mediator between God and humanity by being fully both. Attempts to define Christology starting from either Christ's divinity or from his humanity, doing theology from 'above' or 'below', never quite work.[13] The early Christian Fathers instead started with a concept of Christ's unitary being as both God and man, reflecting their conviction that Christ's priesthood is found neither exclusively in his humanity (as Aquinas, Barth and others have argued) or in his divinity (as some Lutherans, such as Andreas Osiander, held), but in both.[14] Christ had to be both fully human and fully divine to be an effective mediator between humanity and God. In Christ, humanity and divinity are not so much connected, they are united. Divinity takes on humanity, and humanity is infused with divinity.

Christ, priesthood and union with God

This is a point made perhaps most eloquently by John Calvin, possibly the Christian theologian who has most thoroughly explored this idea of Christ as Mediator, making it a central plank of his Christology:

> This will become even clearer if we call to mind that what the Mediator was to accomplish was no common thing. His task was so to restore us to God's grace as to make of the children of men, children of God; of the heirs of Gehenna, heirs of the Heavenly Kingdom. Who could have done this had not the selfsame Son of God become the Son of man, and had not so taken what was ours as to impart what was his to us, and to make what was his by nature ours by grace? Therefore, relying on this pledge, we trust that we are sons of God, for God's natural Son fashioned for himself a body from our body, flesh from our flesh, bones from our bones, that he might be one with us. Ungrudgingly he took our nature upon himself to impart to us what was his, and to become both Son of God and Son of man in common with us.[15]

The Son of God takes on a human body 'in such a way that his divinity and our human nature might by mutual connection grow together'.[16] He brings together in his own person divinity and humanity to enable a kind of union between them. This, Calvin argues, is a priestly function: 'Surely, if he had not come to reconcile God and man, the honour of his priesthood would have fallen away, since a priest is appointed as an intermediary to intercede between God and men.'[17] Christ unites himself with full humanity so that that very humanity can be rescued, redeemed and ultimately perfected.

Calvin's point is that while it is important to preserve the distinction between Creator and Creation, at the same time, the unity of humanity and divinity in Christ, in which Christ is *both* fully divine and fully human, ensures the possibility of real *union* between God and us, and not just relationship. We are perhaps familiar with talk of having a 'personal relationship with God'. This is not untrue – in one sense, we are invited into relationship with God. Yet the goal of Christian life, as Calvin and the Christology of Chalcedon see it, is something greater and more wonderful than this: it is real personal union with God in Christ, or, as the author of 2 Peter puts it, to 'participate in the divine nature' (2 Pet. 1.4). For Calvin, the Holy Spirit unites us with Christ so that we share in the divine embrace between the Father and the Son.[18] The goal of Christian life is not so much a relationship between two parties, but a more intimate union that on the one hand maintains the distinction between the Creator and the Creation, yet also establishes a genuine union between them.[19] This is just what we find in the person of Christ himself, although with the crucial distinction that, in us, this union takes place by grace, not by nature: we are sons and daughters of God by adoption, rather than by natural generation – only the Son has that status.[20]

Calvin makes this point particularly clearly, but he is not alone in doing so. The soteriology which emerged out of the early Eastern Church sees in the incarnation the healing of a diseased human nature, the renovation and cleansing of a corrupted humanity by the entry into it of the divine nature, so that the image of God is restored. As Athanasius puts it, when a picture is damaged, it requires the subject of the portrait to sit again so it can be re-drawn, and in the same way, the divine Son 'came to our region to renew man once made in his likeness'.[21]

More recently, the Scottish theologian T. F. Torrance has brought out a particularly important aspect of this point:

> We must think of Jesus Christ as the Mediator of divine revelation and reconciliation in virtue of what he is in his own personal Identity and Reality. He does not mediate a revelation or a recon-ciliation that is other than what he is, as though he were only the agent or instrument of that mediation to mankind. He embodies what he mediates in himself, for what he mediates and what he is are one and the same. He constitutes in his own incarnate person the content and the reality of what he mediates in both revelation and reconciliation.[22]

Torrance's point is a subtle critique of some misunderstandings of Christology and soteriology. Sometimes we think that the work of Christ was to win for us something other than himself, such as forgiveness, or an objective forensic righteousness. This kind of idea could be presumed from some statements of the sixteenth-century Lutheran Reformers. Luther's concept of 'alien righteousness' – a righteousness won for us by Christ which is received by faith – or Philipp Melanchthon's famous statement 'to know Christ is to know his benefits'[23] could be taken to mean that knowing Christ leads us beyond Christ to the prizes he has won for us.[24] Torrance, along with Calvin, however, insists that what Christ brings us is himself. As the Mediator, he does not mediate to us something other than what he is. Just as he is in his own person the union of God and humanity in a way that preserves the unique identity and value of both, so what he offers us is the possibility of just such a union – being drawn into true participation in God, not just a relationship with him.[25]

At the heart of the notion of the priesthood of Christ is the claim that it is in Christ that humanity meets God, and nowhere else. There is both an inclusiveness and at the same time an exclusiveness about this. It is inclusive in the sense that all humanity is potentially included in this union. The Word assumes human flesh, thus dignifying humanity for all time. Athanasius' image of the king who visits and lives for a while in a city, thus dignifying that city by his presence in it (even though in one particular house within the city), hits exactly this note – that the incarnation makes a difference to the whole of humanity, even if it has to be appropriated by individuals.[26] At the same time this is deeply exclusive in that it stands as a claim that it is in Christ alone that humanity encounters God. It is in Christ's divine–human nature that Christ's priestly ministry is located – that ministry of uniting humanity and divinity, making it possible for humans to share in the divine nature.

Jesus the High Priest

When the letter to the Hebrews, and the later Christian tradition for that matter, calls Jesus Christ the true High Priest, we can now perhaps begin to see a little of what that means. As the Son, he is priestly in that he stands between God and Creation, and in particular between God and humanity, in a way that unites rather than just links the two. He unites divinity and humanity by being both divine and human.

This chapter has explored the significance of the incarnation to the understanding of Christ's priestly character. The priesthood of Christ is both eternal and mediatorial. In the person of Jesus Christ, God unites himself to human nature, making possible an intimate union between them. Christ fully participates in both divine and human nature, so that he is able to bring about a new way of being human. The main way in which the letter to the Hebrews uses the word 'mediator' is to speak of Jesus as the mediator of a new covenant (8.6; 9.15; 12.24), a covenant that involves an internalizing of the divine law, a deeper intimacy that goes beyond the knowledge of the Torah, towards an instinctive obedience from the heart (Heb. 8.8–12; 10.16). The law was so much part of the divine identity that to 'write the law on their hearts' carries with it the implication of a union of mind, soul and will with God himself. This is a new way of life, a new covenant that 'speaks a better word than the blood of Abel' (Heb. 12.24).

This reference to blood highlights another set of ideas connected with the notion of the priesthood of Christ, which refer not so much to his incarnation, but to his death, resurrection and ascension. And it is to these themes that we turn in the next chapter.

2

The priesthood of Christ: ascent

So far we have traced Christ's priesthood in the incarnation. In the coming together of God and humanity in the person of Jesus Christ, the proper nature of both are preserved in a way that enables true union between them, both for him and, in turn, for us. Yet more needs to be said. The picture we are given in Scripture of the priesthood of Christ goes beyond the incarnation itself, to include the whole story of Christ. This chapter will go on to trace how the idea of the priesthood of Christ is filled out in atonement, confirmed in the resurrection and completed in the ascension.

In the 'downward' movement of the incarnation, God, in the form of his Son, assumed human nature in the way we have already explored. Yet the incarnation had to go deeper, into death itself, to remedy not just the ontological difference between God and humanity, but also the moral distance as well – to redeem humanity from its sin and disobedience. In the letter to the Hebrews, the priesthood of Christ is not just related to his identity as the Son, making possible this union between God and humanity, it also is explored further to the point of death. This descent in incarnation, into the reality of not just Creation, but a fallen Creation, takes the ultimate form of crucifixion, of atonement, of the self-offering of a perfect sacrifice.

In the introduction we drew attention to a vital programmatic statement in the early chapters of Hebrews for our understanding of the priesthood of Christ:

> For this reason he had to be made like them, fully human in every
> way, in order that he might become a merciful and faithful high

priest in service to God, and that he might make atonement for the sins of the people. Because he himself suffered when he was tempted, he is able to help those who are being tempted.

(2.17–18)

This text links incarnation with atonement. The Son of God takes on flesh, shares the weakness and frailty of ordinary human nature, not just to unite them in his own being, but to do more: to atone for the sins of the very human race into which he entered.

The crucifixion

Our line of thought so far has dealt with the union of God and humanity in the incarnation, in the descent of the Son into human bodily life. If the world had not fallen, if Creation was in its original state and condition, that presumably would have been enough to unite God and humanity.[1] However, the theology of Hebrews assumes that more needs to be done. With its background in the Jewish sacrificial system, the theology of Hebrews demands that the sin of humanity be dealt with by sacrifice.

As the Son descends, he dies on the cross as the divine and human Son of God, descending into hell as the lowest point of the journey. This sharing of the nature of both is crucial to any doctrine of the atonement. He dies as the divine Son of God, sinless, a perfect offering, God himself, taking on human flesh, entering into the depths of human despair and judgement, to rescue and redeem human nature.

Perfecting

Hebrews uses the imagery of cleansing for the effect of the sacrifice of Christ. His blood cleanses the people: 'the law requires that nearly everything be cleansed with blood, and without the shedding of blood there is no forgiveness' (Heb. 9.22). Three times Hebrews uses the idea of the 'cleansing of the conscience'.[2] Christ's obedient life and death, offered as a sacrifice for the sins of the world, makes the perfect sacrifice that brings cleansing of mind, soul and conscience. The idea here is not so much that of the forgiveness of sins (in fact, the text just mentioned is the only instance of the word 'forgiveness' in the entire letter), as of cleansing from defilement. Sin is seen as that which spoils, dirties or sullies human nature. It is stained and needs cleansing so it can shine in its pristine glory. In other words, it needs to be made perfect, brought to its proper state and fulfilment.

At this point, a further aspect of the priesthood of Christ begins to emerge. So far, we have been exploring the idea of mediation, whereby the Son, combining in himself the natures of humanity and divinity enables a true union between them. Here we begin to see the idea of perfection or perfecting, understood more as a verb than as a noun. In other words, the priesthood of Christ concerns the perfecting of humanity, rescuing it from its damaged, broken and filthy state, bringing it to its proper, cleansed and complete fulfilment, enabling it to become what it was intended to be. The idea of perfection (*teleiōsis*) occurs frequently in the letter to the Hebrews. Sometimes, as we shall see below, it seems to refer to the perfecting of Christ in the resurrection and especially the ascension, but it is also used in connection with the atoning sacrifice of Christ. Christ himself, as the author of salvation, is made 'perfect [*teleiōsai*] through what he suffered' (2.10). He 'learned obedience from what he suffered and, once made perfect [*teleiōtheis*], he became the source of eternal salvation for all who obey him' (5.8–9). Through the self-offering of Christ, both in his life and his death (and as we shall see, continuing on to his resurrection and ascension), he is made perfect. Even the Son needs to go through the process of self-offering through suffering to be made perfect. This is not a static perfection, but a dynamic one, which comes through the journey made by Jesus the priest.

One further crucial point made by the author of the letter is the finality of this sacrifice. Christ's appearance was 'once for all at the culmination of the ages [*hapax epi sunteleia*] to do away sin by the sacrifice of himself' (9.26). Those who have faith in

Christ 'have been made holy through the sacrifice of the body of Jesus Christ once for all' (*ephapax*) (10.10). The contrast between the sacrifice of Christ the Mediator and the Jerusalem priests as intermediaries is one of completeness. The Temple sacrifices are repeated, ongoing, never-ending and can never finally give 'closure', as we would say today. The perfect sacrifice of Christ does bring that closure, and renders those who believe and obey clean, once and for all. Only his sacrifice is perfect (*teleios*) and can bring about completeness or perfection.

Through his life of obedience, his suffering and his death, Christ is made perfect.

It is important to note in passing that we often misunderstand this notion of Christian 'perfection'. We often interpret it in the Platonic sense of lacking imperfection. Perfection for Plato is found in the 'Forms' or 'Ideas', and all other existence is a kind of falling away from that unattainable perfection. In other words, it is defined in a negative way, denoting the lack of error, sin or flaw. Yet the biblical word, *teleios*, is actually better translated 'mature'. This is a positive definition of the word. It is not so much the absence of flaws, but the presence of full, rich maturity of life and wisdom. In Christian terms it is not so much an ontological category but an eschatological one: it is the goal towards which all Creation is moving in the plan and purpose of God, which is revealed in Jesus Christ. The perfection of Jesus is his full maturity. And that is what is offered to God on the cross: a perfect sacrifice.

Offering

In the last chapter, we explored the difference between an intermediary and a mediator. An intermediary is a go-between, a figure who is different and separate from the two parties he or she is seeking to join together. A mediator is one who shares in the nature of the two parties, drawing them together into a closer union. This distinction can help us see the difference between Christ the priest and the cultic priests of the Temple sacrifices. The Jewish priests, entering regularly into the tabernacle to offer sacrifices are in fact intermediaries.[3] Levitical priests certainly did not share the divine nature. They also occupied an ambiguous place with regard to the people of Israel. The priest was regarded as separated from the people, standing apart from the general community as a cultic official; yet, as the author of Hebrews recognized well, the priest has to 'offer sacrifices for his own sins, as well as the sins of the people' (Heb. 5.3). The priest stands as a kind of representative of the people, yet as he does not share the divine nature, he cannot at the same time represent God, and all he can do is offer an imperfect, hopeful sacrifice.[4] As the author of Hebrews sees clearly, what is really needed is a mediator, one who genuinely reconciles and unites the divine and the human, and who offers a perfect sacrifice, one perfected by obedience and suffering, untainted by the priest's own personal failings.

In one sense, Jesus offers a sacrifice as a priest just like those others in the Jerusalem Temple. He shares in the same humanity as them – he makes an offering for sins just as they do. Yet because he is the divine–human Son of God, his priesthood and his sacrifice are different. Ordinary Levitical priests in the Jerusalem Temple always had to offer sacrifice for their own sins as well as for those of the people (7.27–28). In the same way, the sacrifices they offer are themselves imperfect, unable fully to satisfy (10.1, 4). As the author puts it:

> Day after day every priest stands and performs his religious duties; again and again he offers the same sacrifices, which can never take away sins. But when this priest had offered for all time one sacrifice for sins, he sat down at the right hand of God.   (10.11–12)

This distinction between Christ's priesthood and that of the Aaronic priesthood lies in the nature of the life that is offered. Colin Gunton puts it like this:

> There are to be discerned in the baptism and temptations the beginnings of a priestly activity, not of mediating the spirit of the Father to humankind, but the human priestly action of offer-ing to the Father the perfection of a true human life ... Jesus'

particular humanity is perfected by the Spirit who respects his
freedom by enabling him to be what he was called through his
baptism to be.[5]

Christ assumes fallen human flesh, but by the Spirit is enabled
to overcome the temptations and inclinations of that flesh to
offer himself as a perfect obedient sacrifice to the Father: 'Christ,
who through the eternal Spirit offered himself unblemished to
God' (9.14). In the most important sense then, he dies as one of
us. It is precisely as a human that he offers himself:

> For this reason he had to be made like them, fully human in every
> way, in order that he might become a merciful and faithful high
> priest in service to God, and that he might make atonement for
> the sins of the people.   (2.17)

Because it is humanity that has sinned, it is humanity that has
to make atonement for that sin, and in Christ, the divine Son,
there is found a human being capable of making that atonement.
This is precisely because he has no sin of his own to atone for:

> Such a high priest truly meets our need – one who is holy, blame-
> less, pure, set apart from sinners, exalted above the heavens. Unlike
> the other high priests, he does not need to offer sacrifices day after
> day, first for his own sins, and then for the sins of the people. He
> sacrificed for their sins once for all when he offered himself. For
> the law appoints as high priests men in all their weakness; but the
> oath, which came after the law, appointed the Son, who has been
> made perfect for ever.   (7.26–28)

Yet at the same time, his divine nature is also crucial to this sacrifice. If he were not enabled by his full participation in the Spirit
to offer himself to the Father, if he were not 'the exact representation of his being' (1.3), then he could not offer such a perfect
sacrifice. It is because of who he is that his sacrifice is effective.
In the mind of the author of the letter, there is a deep continuity
between Christ's life of obedience and his death on the cross. 'Son
though he was, he learned obedience from what he suffered and,

once made perfect, he became the source of eternal salvation for all who obey him' (5.8). It is not that his death alone achieves satisfaction for sin, but that it is precisely the offering of this particular human life that achieves salvation.[6]

It is by the self-offering of himself to God as a sacrifice through the whole of his earthly obedience, culminating on the cross, that Christ offers a perfect sacrifice for sin. This link between Christ's life and his death, between incarnation and atonement, person and work is emphasized throughout the theological tradition. Athanasius writes: 'The Word being Fashioner of all, afterwards was made High Priest by putting on a body which was originate and made, and such as can make an offering for us.'[7] His point is that the divine *Logos* took on human flesh in order to make the offering for sin that was required. Christ takes on human flesh in order to offer sacrifice as a priest. The result is that Christ was able to offer a perfect human sacrifice for sin. It is as a full human being, one of us, sharing in flesh and blood, just like ours, that he offers himself for the sins of the world.

Calvin, developing his Christology of mediation, puts it like this:

> Now someone asks, How has Christ abolished sin, banished the separation between us and God, and acquired righteousness to render God favourable and kindly toward us? To this we can in general reply that he has achieved this for us by the whole course of his obedience . . . Yet to define the way of salvation more exactly, Scripture ascribes this as peculiar and proper to Christ's death.[8]

In the incarnation, the Word takes on human flesh. In the crucifixion, the Word descends to the lowest point of all, offering himself to the Father as a sinless sacrifice. He dies on our behalf, as one of us, offering a perfect human life to the Father to deal with sin once and for all, as the true priest. Christ the Mediator binds broken human nature to himself, lives a perfected human life and then offers that perfected humanity to God as a gift.

As such, Christ enacts the ultimate and final act of worship. Worship, sacrifice and offering were always bound up together, both in Old Testament Temple-based religion, and also in first-century paganism, with its own repeated offerings of sacrifices to the gods at their local temples. Christ's sacrifice is not just another act of worship, it is the final act of worship, the offering of a perfect sacrifice to end all sacrifices.

It is important to grasp one key distinction here, however. The self-offering of Christ is the only sufficient sacrifice for sins. Yet in the Old Testament there were many kinds of sacrifice – not just those made on the Day of Atonement for the sins of the people. There were guilt offerings, fellowship offerings, wave offerings and offerings of thanksgiving.[9] Offering was not just about atonement, it was also about worship. As we will see later, while Christ's sacrifice for sin can never be repeated or added to, the notion of offering sacrifices as worship, 'offer[ing] your bodies as a living sacrifice' (Rom. 12.1) for example, still continues in Christian worship. Hebrews insists that Christ's sacrifice for sin is final and complete. At the same time, the Church does still continually offer the 'sacrifice of praise' (Heb. 13.15).

Resurrection

The next stage on the journey of Jesus the priest is the resurrection. Having offered himself as a sacrifice for the sins of the world, Christ is raised to live for ever. It has often been noticed that while the incarnation, cross and ascension feature frequently in the theology of the letter to the Hebrews, the resurrection is less obvious.[10] However, there are a number of places where the idea of resurrection does feature significantly in this story of Jesus the priest.

David Moffitt has argued that Jesus' priesthood in the letter to the Hebrews is closely connected to his resurrection.[11] The two places where Psalm 110 is quoted in the letter both imply that Christ became a priest through the resurrection. As we saw a few pages ago, the author of Hebrews says that Christ was heard because of his reverent submission. Son though he was, he learned obedience from what he suffered and, once made perfect, he became the source of eternal salvation for all who obey him, and was designated by God to be high priest in the order of Melchizedek. (5.7–10)

This 'being made perfect', coming after the mention of his suffering, seems to refer to his vindication and the consummation of his life in the resurrection. It implies that it was through the resurrection that his priestly ability to be the 'source of eternal salvation', the 'high priest in the order of Melchizedek' comes about.

Similarly, Moffitt argues, Christ is also said to have become a priest in the order of Melchizedek, not through his ancestry, like the Aaronic priests, having been born into a particular tribe or family, but instead through 'the power of an indestructible life' (7.16). The contrast is deliberately stark. While the claim to priesthood of an Aaronic priest is grounded in his birth into the tribe and line of Aaron, the claim of Christ to be the true priest is grounded instead in his 'indestructible life', which seems a clear reference to his resurrection.

Revealing

Does this mean therefore that Christ becomes High Priest at the resurrection? This is where the Christology of Wolfhart Pannenberg, with its emphasis on the resurrection, helps us. For Pannenberg, the true significance of Jesus Christ is revealed only at the resurrection: 'From Jesus' resurrection, light is shed backward upon his earthly life that reveals its true significance.'[12] The resurrection is the pivotal point of the story of Christ for Pannenberg because it is there that divine confirmation is finally and decisively given that Jesus truly is the sinless Son of God, whose sacrifice cleanses us from our sins. Indeed, it is only in the light of the resurrection that we can see that Jesus is the true Son, the one whose sacrifice was acceptable, and whose life was sinless and innocent. The resurrection reveals Christ as the true High Priest.

There were, of course, many other claimants to messiahship around the time of Jesus. If God had raised Simon of Peraea, or Jesus son of Saphias from Tiberias, or Simon Bar Kochba or any other such controversial contemporary figure, then that would have been the definitive sign that *they* were the true messiah, the chosen one; it would have been *their* life and message that was vindicated by God – in a sense *they* would henceforth have been seen as the Son of God, which at the time seems to have been a messianic title.

And yet, it was Jesus of Nazareth, this particular man, who was raised from the dead as the first fruits of the coming resurrection. The resurrection is the true vindication of Jesus. Because of the resurrection, we look back on his life differently. If he had not been raised it is very unlikely that we would still be talking and writing about him now, or that the epistle to the Hebrews would have been written at all. Without the resurrection, he would have been consigned to history as another failed claimant to be the one sent from God, and any claim to divine Sonship or sinlessness, or to be the divine–human Mediator would have been soon discounted. As Pannenberg put it boldly: 'Apart from the resurrection from the dead, Jesus would not be God, even though from the perspective of the resurrection he is retrospectively one with God in his whole pre-Easter life.'[13] What Pannenberg means is not that Jesus 'became' the Son of God at the resurrection, but that the resurrection establishes God's verdict on his life and confirms its true significance.[14]

It has to be said that Pannenberg does not make much of the priestly office of Christ.[15] Nonetheless, it is possible to apply these thoughts to the notion of the priesthood of Christ. Further on in chapter 7 of the letter to the Hebrews, the author contrasts the Aaronic priesthood with that of Jesus:

> Now there have been many of those priests, since death prevented them from continuing in office; but because Jesus lives for ever, he has a permanent priesthood. Therefore he is able to save completely those who come to God through him, because he always lives to intercede for them. (7.23–25)

This text, with its mention of 'many . . . priests [whose] death prevented them from continuing in office' contrasts Jesus with other high priests in the history of Israel. In a sense, each of these might have had a claim to be the eternal Priest of God. If God had raised Caiaphas, or Jonathan ben Ananus, his successor, from death, they would have been seen as the true High Priest who lives for ever. Yet it was Jesus of Nazareth who was raised, so that, despite the absence of a genealogical connection with Aaron, it is Jesus, not Caiaphas or Jonathan, who is the true High Priest, able to save those who come to God through him. Despite its shameful nature, it is his death, not theirs, that is seen as the sacrifice for sins, the Passover offering that surpasses all other Passover offerings. Without the resurrection, his death on the cross could have no claim to be the sacrifice for sins, but instead would only be another tragic miscarriage of justice, another instance of the triumph of violence over meekness.

Confirming

As Pannenberg helps us see, it is in this sense that the resurrection establishes and confirms the priesthood of Christ. Because God raised this man and no other from the dead, we see his life and identity completely differently. His true identity as the priestly Mediator, the divine Son of God, uniting humanity and divinity in one person is revealed. The character of his death as a sacrifice for sins is confirmed. The resurrection constitutes Christ's priesthood not in the sense that he becomes a priest in the resurrection, but that it establishes and confirms his priesthood, so we can see that his life was truly the life of the divine–human Mediator, and his death a sacrifice that finally deals with human sin once and for all: that he is both priest and victim. So when Hebrews says 'because Jesus lives for ever, he has a permanent priesthood' (7.24), we can see that the resurrection casts a light both backwards and forwards, onto Christ's priestly character in his life and also his ongoing priestly ministry in the future and in eternity. We know that Christ is the true High Priest because of his resurrection.

Ascension

Christ is priest in his incarnation, in that he is the divine–human Son of God who unites humanity and God in himself. He exercises his priesthood on the cross, as he offers his own perfect life as a sacrifice for sins, to redeem and cleanse humanity from its slavery and defilement. That priesthood is then confirmed and established in the resurrection. Finally, it is completed and consummated in the ascension.

The ascension features strongly in the letter to the Hebrews. The first few verses speak of how 'after he had provided purification for sins, he sat down at the right hand of the Majesty in heaven' (1.3). Later in the letter, we find the description of Jesus as a High Priest who supplies exactly what we need: 'one who is holy, blameless, pure, set apart from sinners, exalted above the heavens' (7.26). We have a High Priest who 'sat down at the right hand of the throne of the Majesty in heaven' (8.1). Christ 'entered heaven itself, now to appear for us in God's presence' (9.24). He is 'the pioneer and perfecter of our faith. For the joy that was set before him he endured the cross, scorning its shame, and sat down at the right hand of the throne of God' (12.2).

Interceding

The consummation of the priesthood of Christ is found in the ascension. In his exaltation to the right hand of the Father in heaven, in his mediatorial role, he now intercedes for us. The crucified, risen and ascended Christ 'is able to save completely those who come to God through him, because he always lives to intercede for them' (7.25). The deepest pastoral implication of the doctrine of the priesthood of Christ is stated in the letter to the Hebrews in this way:

> Therefore, since we have a great high priest who has ascended into heaven, Jesus the Son of God, let us hold firmly to the faith we profess. For we do not have a high priest who is unable to feel sympathy for our weaknesses, but we have one who has been

tempted in every way, just as we are – yet he did not sin. Let us then
approach God's throne of grace with confidence, so that we may
receive mercy and find grace to help us in our time of need.

(4.14–16)

Christ, as the true High Priest, the Mediator between God and
humanity, the one who offers his own life as a sacrifice for sins, and
whose priesthood is confirmed by the resurrection from the dead
now sits at the right hand of God, interceding for us.

Yet there is one particular aspect of this that demands close
attention. Christ ascended to the Father precisely *as one of us.*
He is one who 'has been tempted in every way, just as we are'.
His intercession for us is based on his likeness to us. Because
of his sharing the nature of God, he can properly sit at the right
hand of the Father; because he shares our nature, and because
he has suffered in his body as we do, he is able to intercede for
us. The statement in 9.24 that he 'entered heaven itself, now to
appear *for us* in God's presence' emphasizes this same point,
that in the person of Christ, humanity itself has ascended to the
right hand of the Father. This is the final, glorious conclusion of
the story of the priesthood of Christ: that he, sharing our nature,
as a full human being, sits at the right hand of the Father. The
ascension therefore speaks of the fulfilment of human destiny.
Just as God in Christ has united himself with human nature
in the incarnation, offered himself in the person of his Son as
a sacrifice for sins, so he has now raised human nature to its
proper place at his right hand in heaven. The ascension signifies
the final destiny of humanity – to be raised with Christ, drawn
back into full fellowship with God, in even closer intimacy with
God than Adam experienced in Eden. Adam knew the presence
of God, but not participation in God. Until the incarnation,
that could not be conceivable, especially so after the fall. The
ascension completes the full restoration and destiny of humanity,
reconciled to God in the person and through the work of Christ
the Mediator.

Exalting

Douglas Farrow, in his fine book on the theme, contrasts two different understandings of ascension in Christian theology. One is a strand rooted in Origen and running through to Schleiermacher, which essentially sees the ascension as a spiritual event, the raising of the mind or spirit to God, as a kind of escape from the flesh. Jesus ascends in his 'spiritual' nature not his physical body, which is left behind. On the other hand there is what Farrow sees as the biblical doctrine of the ascension, expressed most fully in Irenaeus, who sees the ascension as the raising of this particular man Jesus Christ to the right hand of the Father, in his full bodily humanity. Irenaeus envisages an ascension of the body, not just of the mind or the spirit. This is the exaltation of humanity in its fullness into the presence of God. This provides the template, or the pattern, for God's dealing with us now and in the future: 'In the ascension, God does something new with and for the man Jesus, as a basis of that which he intends ultimately to do with and for us.'[16]

It is not just that he is ascended and exalted: we are ascended and exalted with him, 'bringing many sons and daughters to glory' (Heb. 2.10). This trajectory – downwards in the incarnation, to the depths of the cross, then upwards in resurrection and finally fulfilled in ascension – is the story of how in the person of the Son, God stoops down to join himself with created and sinful humanity, perfects that humanity through suffering obedience, offers it back to God as a sacrifice for sins, then raises it to where it truly belongs, at the right hand of the Father, so that those who are in Christ might be perfected, might become what they were always intended to be: united with God, enjoying full, unbroken fellowship with God their Creator.

The pastoral implications of the ascended priesthood of Christ are laid out in chapters 9 and 10 of the letter to the Hebrews. Because Christ has entered the most holy place, access is made possible for human beings to do the same. It becomes possible for human beings to ascend to the right hand of the Father, cleansed of sin and purified in conscience:

> Since we have a great high priest over the house of God, let us draw near to God with a sincere heart and with the full assurance that faith brings, having our hearts sprinkled to cleanse us from a guilty conscience, and having our bodies washed with pure water.
>
> (10.21–22)

The ascension completes the possibility opened up for humanity to become what it was always intended to be: pure, spotless, participating in God's nature, a little lower than the angels, with the full dignity and honour it was always intended to have.

As we saw earlier, Hebrews speaks of Christ as being 'made perfect' through suffering. However, he is finally perfected in the ascension where he is exalted to the right hand of the father. The author uses this language of 'being made perfect' as a kind of circumlocution for ascension to become the High Priest: 'once made perfect, he became the source of eternal salvation for all who obey him and was designated by God to be high priest in the order of Melchizedek' (5.9–10). The Son has now 'been made perfect for ever' (7.28). The Christian's gaze is now fixed on the ascended Jesus: 'we . . . see Jesus, who was made lower than the angels for a little while, now crowned with glory and honour because he suffered death' (2.9). He is now the mediator of a new covenant, who serves in the heavenly sanctuary (8.2), entering the most holy place by his own blood (9.12). Yet the purpose of this making perfect of Christ through suffering does not end there: its purpose is the perfecting of us human beings: 'By one sacrifice he has made perfect for ever those who are being made holy' (10.14). The trajectory of the story ends not just with the ascension and perfecting of Christ, but the perfecting of all those who are in Christ, the communion of saints (11.40), the 'spirits of the righteous made perfect' (12.23).

Closely tied to ascension, of course, is the gift of the Holy Spirit. The Spirit is given by the ascended Christ, and in a sense can only be given once Christ has ascended (John 16.7). The Spirit comes to universalize the presence of the ascended Christ: we do not have Christ's body with us here now – it is located at the right hand of the Father – but we do have his presence by the Holy Spirit. And of course it is the Spirit who is particularly connected with the work of the perfecting of Creation, as the early Fathers saw very clearly.[17] As Basil the Great put it, 'The Originator of all things . . . creates through the Son and perfects through the Spirit.'[18] It is by the Spirit that Christ is enabled to offer himself up to the Father (Heb. 9.14). As Colin Gunton writes: 'Jesus' particular humanity is perfected by the Spirit who respects his freedom by enabling him to be what he was called through his baptism to be.'[19] Jesus himself is perfected in his humanity by the very same Spirit who will bring all Creation to perfection, and it is by that same Spirit that the Son is enabled to perfect humanity in a way that can be offered to the Father.

Christ and true priesthood

We have completed our Christological journey through the letter to the Hebrews, exploring how Christ as the true High Priest brings us to God. As we look back, we might ask the question: At what point does Christ become a priest? Is it in the incarnation? The cross? The resurrection? The ascension?

Different parts of the letter suggest different answers to this question. One early statement – 'he had to be made like them, fully human in every way, in order that he might become a merciful and faithful high priest in service to God' (2.17) – seems to point to the incarnation as the vital moment. Another – 'once made perfect, he became the source of eternal salvation for all who obey him and was designated by God to be high priest in the order of Melchizedek' (5.9–10) – indicates either the resurrection or the ascension. Yet another – 'when Christ came as high priest of the good things that are now already here, he went through the greater and more perfect tabernacle . . . he entered . . . by his own blood'

(9.11–12) – points to the cross, the moment of the shedding of his blood. Then again there is this: '. . . behind the curtain, where our forerunner, Jesus, has entered on our behalf. He has become a high priest for ever' (6.19–20), which seems to point to the ascension as the vital moment.

In other words, it is hard to pinpoint one particular moment, whether incarnation, cross, resurrection or ascension as the precise time or instance at which Christ becomes High Priest. Perhaps the key to this is 5.5:

> Christ did not take on himself the glory of becoming a high priest. But God said to him, 'You are my Son; today I have become your Father.' And he says in another place, 'You are a priest for ever, in the order of Melchizedek.'

Christ's priesthood is parallel to his Sonship. His priesthood is an eternal priesthood, yet it is played out in the dramatic narrative of his incarnation, death, resurrection and ascension. It is the whole trajectory of the story that builds and fills out his identity as High Priest.

This is why the letter to the Hebrews points to all four of these 'Acts' in the divine drama of redemption as key moments in the priestly identity of Jesus. In a sense, they fill out for us what priesthood actually means and enable us to draw these threads together into a fuller picture of what priesthood, defined by Christ the true High Priest, is and does.

Calvin writes: 'the salvation of all of us is effected and turns on the priesthood of Christ'.[20] In other words, Christ's priesthood refers to the way in which salvation happens – the *ordo salutis*. God's interaction with the world is always mediated through Christ, never outside him. God the Father creates and redeems the world through the Son. Likewise, we never approach the Father immediately. We only approach him through the Son, in this mediated manner, through Christ. God's desire is to bless his world. And as Calvin also reminds us, those blessings are focused in a particular place: in Christ. It is in and through Christ that God blesses the world, through his descent in incarnation and atonement to redeem and rescue Creation, and his ascent through resurrection and ascension to restore it to God.

Summary and conclusion

At the risk of simplification, we might say that priesthood, as understood through Christ, consists of the following three elements:

1 *Mediating*: Christ as priest mediates between God and the world, sharing the nature of both, uniting both God and Creation in his one person. The Son descends into Creation, uniting human nature with himself, taking identification to the point of the cross. He overcomes the barrier that stands between God and his Creation, so that the two are united in a deep intimacy.

   As such, he alone *intercedes* for us at the right hand of the Father, representing us before God, and yet sharing in the intimacy of a common nature with the Father in the Spirit. Christ stands between us and God, bringing God to us and representing us to God.

2 *Perfecting*: Christ as priest perfects Creation, and particularly the human part of it. In other words, he is the chosen one, who brings the rest of humanity, the rest of Creation to its perfected state. It is his calling to enable Creation to become all that it was intended to be.

   As such, Christ brings the *blessing* of God to bear on his Creation. Creation comes into being in the beginning, yet needs the continual divine blessing for it to become all that it has the potential to be. This is the priestly task of blessing, bringing completion and joy to the world.

3 *Offering*: Christ the Priest *offers* this perfected human life as a gift, a sacrifice, back to God, consummating Creation by offering it back, connecting it to the very God from whom it came, perfected in glory, exalted to the right hand of God,

healed, restored, finally satisfied. This offering is accepted and completed in the resurrection.

As such Christ performs the true act of *worship*, offering himself as a 'living sacrifice' (Rom. 12.1). He is the true worshipper, the only real worship leader, in whom all our worship is offered to the Father.[21]

Priesthood can be described therefore as the irreducibly personal way in which God relates to the world. There are, of course, other mediating elements within Creation that mediate God's will and blessing to Creation, such as time and space themselves. These, however, are not priestly because they are not personal – they do not reflect Christ the true High Priest who is himself nothing less than personal. In the following chapters we will explore how Christ's priesthood, his mediating, perfecting and offering, is enacted in the world through other persons, made in his image and called to be the channel of the grace and blessing of God in Christ to the world.

One last point: the letter to the Hebrews focuses on the perfecting of humanity as the goal of Christ's priestly identity and work. And yet there are hints of something more. In the context of writing of Jesus, the mediator of a new covenant, the author adds:

> Now he has promised, 'Once more I will shake not only the earth but also the heavens.' The words 'once more' indicate the [transformation][22] of what can be shaken – that is, created things – so that what cannot be shaken may remain.   (12.26–27)

The story goes even beyond the redemption of humanity to the transformation of the whole of Creation, to a removal of what stains and disrupts the heavens and the earth, and the final establishment of an order than cannot be shaken. As Wolfhart Pannenberg puts it: 'as the Son he brings the entire creation into the obedience of Sonship, thereby mediating it into immediacy to the Father'.[23]

This allusion towards the end of the work mirrors a similar reference to Creation at its start, to Creation as being made through the Son. The priestly work of Christ begins with a world made through Christ, and ends in a world redeemed, cleansed and restored through the mediation of Christ.

Yet how does all this happen? Up to this point, this discussion could all seem a little abstract or metaphysical. It could seem as if it is located on a plane of spiritual reality far removed from the actual day-to-day experience of life, particularly Christian life. The rest of this book begins to flesh out how this priesthood of Christ is played out within the ordinary, yet extraordinary, world in which we live, within the very fabric of family, church, politics, calling and relationships, in a circle of blessing of which the circumference widens the more we see how generous and expansive the love of God is.

3

Priesthood questioned

Christ is the true High Priest. It sounds straightforward, but when you think of it, this claim is not without its difficulty. It is exclusive. Awkwardly so. It suggests that he is the *only* High Priest, the only Mediator. It claims that the Old Testament priesthood has now been fulfilled and completed in the coming of Christ the High Priest, of whom all previous high priests were merely anticipatory echoes. As one of the early Pauline writings puts it: 'there is one God; there is also one mediator between God and humankind, Christ Jesus, himself human, who gave himself a ransom for all' (1 Tim. 2.5, NRSV).

In the letter to the Hebrews, Jesus Christ is the Son of God in human flesh, the one who unites humanity and divinity in his own person, who offers his own sinless life for the sins of the world, who is raised by the Father as a confirmation and establishment of that priestly identity and who is now raised to the right hand of the same Father to intercede as Mediator for those he represents. The point is, of course, that all of these functions or acts are unique. No one else, by definition, can do these things. As we saw in our discussion of the resurrection, God raised *this* man and no other. He raised *this* man to his right hand on high. There is no other priest, no other mediator.

Elsewhere in the New Testament, the word 'priest', or *hiereus*, occurs most often in reference to the priests in the Temple in Jerusalem, or the high priest himself. In the Gospels, in fact, this is the only way the word is used. In the book of Acts, this pattern continues, although the word is also expanded to describe priests at pagan temples, such as the priest of Zeus in Lystra who brings a couple of bulls to offer in sacrifice to Paul and Barnabas, assuming them to be semi-divine figures capable of divine acts of healing. Priests were therefore part of the furniture of first-century religion, both Jewish and pagan, a familiar concept to the writers and readers of the New Testament, no matter what their religious background.

Having said all that, although it was written against the back-ground of various kinds of priesthood, nowhere in the New Testament do we find Christian liturgical officials, or church leaders, referred to by the name 'priest'. These early Christian writers steadfastly refuse to designate any one individual within the Church with the title 'priest', apart from, as we have seen, Jesus Christ himself.

That might seem the end of the story. If Jesus christ is the true Mediator, there can be no other, and further discussion of priesthood presumably comes to an end. If there is one mediator between God and humanity, then there is no need for any more. Surely Christ is sufficient to bridge the gap between God and Creation?

Yet this is not the only way the early Christians spoke of priest-liness. As it happens, despite this emphasis on the unique standing of Christ as the true High Priest, as the only Mediator between God and humanity, the New Testament does actually talk about priesthood in a number of other ways. In particular, it suggests that Christ's priesthood is in a sense shared with the Church.

In the Old Testament, Israel was often spoken of as a priestly nation. We have already touched on Israel's identity as a 'kingdom of priests' in Exodus 19. Israel's calling, as we saw there, was not to privilege but to responsibility, to play this role of being 'a covenant for the people, and a light for the Gentiles, to open the eyes that are blind, to free captives from prison and to release from the dungeon those who sit in darkness' (Isa. 42.6–7). Particularly in the prophetic writings of the sixth century BC, Israel plays this role of mediating God's light and healing to the world, the light of God shining among the darkness of the nations. This is why, later in the same text, Israel, despite having its own specific priestly caste in the tribe of Aaron, is explicitly called a priestly nation:

> And you will be called priests of the LORD,
>> you will be named ministers of our God.
> You will feed on the wealth of nations,
>> and in their riches you will boast.
> Instead of your shame
>> you will receive a double portion,
> and instead of disgrace
>> you will rejoice in your inheritance.
> And so you will inherit a double portion in your land,
>> and everlasting joy will be yours.   (Isa. 61.6–7)

Now we might have thought that as the New Testament (or at least the letter to the Hebrews) sees Old Testament priestliness as fulfilled in Christ, focusing this idea of God's mediation onto the person of Christ alone, that the idea of God's people as being priestly would have faded from the scene. However, this does not happen. At the start of this chapter, we saw the text from 1 Timothy, with its language of 'one mediator between God and humankind, Christ Jesus' emphasizing the uniqueness of the priesthood of Christ. Look back a few verses and we find this:

> First of all, then, I urge that supplications, prayers, intercessions, and thanksgivings be made for everyone, for kings and all who are in high positions, so that we may lead a quiet and peaceable life in all godliness and dignity. This is right and is acceptable in the sight of God our Saviour, who desires everyone to be saved and to come to the knowledge of the truth. For there is one God; there is also one mediator between God and humankind, Christ Jesus, himself human, who gave himself a ransom for all.
>
> (1 Tim. 2.1–6, NRSV)

Directly before this uncompromising statement of the unique mediatory role of Christ comes this request that the Church play a mediatory role towards the state. Just as Christ intercedes for humanity to the Father, so the Church, under Timothy's leadership, is also to intercede for humanity to the Father, especially for the social functions represented in government. The first letter of Peter also applies this same language to the Church:

> You are a chosen people, a royal priesthood, a holy nation, God's special possession, that you may declare the praises of him who called you out of darkness into his wonderful light.   (1 Pet. 2.9)

The book of Revelation, like 1 Peter, also applies priestly language to the Church: it is a 'kingdom and priests' to serve God (1.6; 5.10). Similarly, the martyrs are said to be 'priests of God and of Christ and will reign with him for a thousand years' (20.6). There is one other usage of the word in Romans 15.16, to refer to Paul's evangelistic ministry to the Gentiles, which we will look at in more detail later on.

In other words, despite the emphasis on the unique priesthood of Christ, his priesthood seems also to be shared, or expressed, in and through the Church. Now this transition needs exploring more closely. The rest of this book seeks to argue that this notion of priesthood is a vital category for understanding God's way in the world, that Christ's priestly work is played out through other 'priestly' activity. But before we begin to sketch that out, we need to dig deeper into the way in which priesthood has been understood in the Church and, in particular, a tension in the use of the term that runs through its history.

The critique of priesthood

It wasn't long before the Christian Church began to use the language of priesthood (*hiereus* in Greek or *sacerdos* in Latin) for its ministers. In the early centuries, the predominant term was *presbuteros*. Early Christian theologians, such as Clement of Alexandria, Ignatius and Irenaeus, tended to avoid the language of priesthood for Christian ministers. The term *hiereus* only begins to be used of bishops (primarily) towards the end of the second century. The first letter of Clement, written around AD 96, for example, sees the Old Testament priesthood as a prefigurement of New Testament ministry.[1] Tertullian uses the equivalent Latin term '*sacerdos*' to refer to bishops around the same period in his *De Baptismo*. For Cyprian in the third century, the bishop in his priestly role is the normal eucharistic president, although both he and Augustine emphasize the involvement of the whole Christian community in the Eucharist.[2] As bishops came to oversee more than just one congregation and subsequently larger geographical areas, much of their local functions devolved to presbyters, who increasingly presided at the Eucharist in local congregations. During the second century, Christian teachers such as Tertullian and Cyprian begin to link the Christian presbyterate to Old Testament ideas of priesthood, as these were the people who conducted the main acts of worship in the community, focused around the Eucharist.

By the early third century, the presidency at the Eucharist was increasingly focused around, and reserved for, a sacerdotal figure.[3] A little later, Jerome more explicitly linked priesthood to sacrifice. Serious work on the theology and practice of the priesthood begins in the fourth century with writings such as John Chrysostom's *Six Books on the Priesthood*,[4] or Ambrose's *Treatise on Priesthood* from AD 391. Gregory the Great's *Pastoral Care* from two hundred years later connects priesthood to the incarnation, yet still treats priesthood as a primarily pastoral function – it is a work mainly about how pastoral care is exercised through preaching.

In the Middle Ages, such discussion takes on a different tone. Aquinas sees the daily sacrifice of the Eucharist as a commemoration of the priestly offering of Christ, who is the source of all priesthood. Like many medieval writers, ironically, Aquinas is reticent to call Christ by the title of 'priest', preferring other titles, perhaps because of the rise in prominence of ecclesiastical priesthood.[5] Works such as Catherine of Siena's *Dialogue* of 1378 go further, arguing that as the blood of Christ is entrusted to the priests, so they should be treated with deep respect and obedience, so much so that a sin or complaint against priests, whatever their sins, is a sin or complaint against God – a rather dangerous idea in the light of more recent experience!

Meanwhile the actual practice of priesthood had changed over this period. The Gregorian reforms of the eleventh century were a significant moment, as they sought to make priesthood a distinct and separate condition over against the laity, freeing the priest from worldly matters, enabling him to serve God and the Church. The twelfth century saw a revolution in priesthood, with a stricter expectation of a celibate priesthood, free from the demands of wife and children; the requirement that candidates for the priesthood be freeborn, not serfs; and changes that led to priests being less financially beholden to wealthy lay patrons. The Fourth Lateran Council of 1215 insisted that everyone confess to a priest at least once a year and receive Communion from the same priests every Easter. The formal adoption at the same Council of transubstantiation as the official teaching of the Church on how the bread and wine convey the body and blood of Christ likewise gave a heightened importance to the priest. Even though official theology, of course, never claimed that the priest was Christ on earth, the priests' control of access to the body and blood of Christ and the remission of sins, as well as their increasing separation from the laity, gave a different feel towards priesthood in the popular imagination in 1500 than had existed in 1100.[6]

These changes established a greater focus on the sacraments as channelling the grace of Christ to the Christian, and a liberation of the priest to play this central role within the Church of ministering the grace of Christ to the penitent in the mass, through penance and all the other sacraments of the Church. The priest was duly authorized by standing in line with the apostles themselves, receiving Christ's authority handed down through them and their successors, to be the conduit of grace to the Church, to enable the Church as a whole to have access to Christ, present in sacramental form. If the Church is not organically connected to Christ, then how can it be what it is called to be? The reality was that in practice, it often led to an increasingly distant priesthood, elevated above the laity in popular imagination, and hence to a downgrading of the idea of the priesthood of the whole Church, in favour of the priesthood of priests.

These tendencies and this usage began to be tested by a severe critique in the early sixteenth century. What became known as the Reformation was a theological and ecclesiastical movement that had at its heart an emphasis on the uniqueness of Christ. Of all the Reformation slogans, *solus Christus* is perhaps the most central. The Reformation was a recalling of the Church to the notion that God is revealed uniquely in Christ, not in some generalized natural theology; that salvation is found through faith in Christ, not in human striving and effort; that the head of the Church is Christ, rather than any pope or bishop. Along with this, of course, came an emphasis, which we have already seen in Calvin, on Christ as the true Mediator between God and humanity.

It is vital to recognize that, despite the impression sometimes given, the Reformation did not mount an attack on the concept of priesthood. In fact, it could be argued that it was a central category for the Reformers, both in Christology and ecclesiology. When it came to ecclesiology, the Reformation critique of priesthood did not argue on the basis of the priesthood of Christ that no one else could be a priest, but rather that everyone was a priest. Their point was not to deny the possibility of priesthood being extended to others, but to expand it to the whole people of God. Their gripe was not with the idea of priesthood in the Church, but the restriction of the category to the clergy alone.

Luther on priesthood

Martin Luther, in his influential treatise *On the Babylonian Captivity of the Church*, published in 1520, argued that baptism, not ordination, is the basis for all Christian ministry. As a result, 'we are all consecrated priests through baptism'.[7] He takes the point further to say:

It follows from this argument that there is no true, basic difference between laymen and priests, princes and bishops, between religious and secular, except for the sake of office and work, but not for the sake of status. They are all of the spiritual estate, all are truly priests, bishops, and popes.[8]

This was Luther's programmatic statement on priesthood, which caused shock waves around Europe, not least leading to the more egalitarian agenda of the Peasants' Revolt of the early 1520s, an agenda that Luther did not wholly support and which led him to emphasize a more clerical form of ministry in his later thinking. However, the critique of ministerial priesthood developed more fully in his writings over the next few years, coming to a head in his 1523 work *Concerning the Ministry*. This is Luther's essential critique of the Roman idea of priesthood: 'Christ is a priest, therefore Christians are priests . . . we are priests, as he is Priest, sons as he is Son, kings as he is King.'[9]

Luther's conception of the priesthood of Christ focuses on one particular aspect of the trajectory of priesthood that we traced in the last two chapters – his sacrifice on the cross. Drawing on the theology of Christ's priesthood developed in the letter to the Hebrews, Luther continues:

The gospel and all of Scripture present Christ as the high priest, who alone and once for all by offering himself has taken away the sins of all men and accomplished their sanctification for all eternity. For once and for all he entered into the holy place through his own blood, thus securing an eternal redemption [Heb. 9:12, 28; 10:12, 14]. Thus no other sacrifice remains for our sins than his, and, by putting our trust altogether in it, we are saved from sin without any merits or works of our own. Of this sacrifice and offering he has instituted a perpetual remembrance in that he intends to have it proclaimed in the sacrament of the altar and thereby have faith in it strengthened.[10]

This, therefore, is Luther's account of Christ's priesthood. He contrasts Christ's priestly character with that of ordained priests in the medieval Church:

For a priest, especially in the New Testament, was not made but was born. He was created, not ordained. He was born not indeed of flesh, but through a birth of the Spirit, by water and Spirit in the washing of regeneration (John 3:6f.; Titus 3:5f.). Indeed, all Christians are priests, and all priests are Christians. Worthy of anathema is any assertion that a priest is anything else than a Christian.[11]

Only Christ is the true High Priest, in that only he has died for the sins of the world, offering the one sufficient sacrifice to atone for sin. Luther does discern a range of priestly functions in the Church, but his main point is that none of these can or should be restricted to a certain caste of ordained ministers. Instead, they are the possession of the whole Church.

For Luther, the gospel centres on the Word of God that promises grace, forgiveness and divine favour in Christ, to be met by faith. As a result, everything that happens in church should also centre around the ministry of that word in both preached and sacramental form. The main function of Christian priesthood is therefore the ministry of the word, although for Luther, this means much more than preaching. He lists seven principal parts of priestly ministry. The first is to preach and proclaim the promise; the second is to baptize; the third, to administer bread and wine; the fourth, to bind and loose from sin; the fifth, to sacrifice (not in the sense of eucharistic sacrifice, but in the sense of the sacrifice of self and body as in Romans 12.1); the sixth, to pray and intercede for others; and the seventh, to pass on the doctrines of the faith to others. All these tasks he sees as the responsibility of all Christians, and therefore all Christians are caught up in this priestly calling in the Church:

> Here we take our stand: There is no other Word of God than that which is given all Christians to proclaim. There is no other baptism than the one which any Christian can bestow. There is no other remembrance of the Lord's Supper than that which any Christian can observe and which Christ has instituted. There is no other kind of sin than that which any Christian can bind or loose. There is

no other sacrifice than of the body of every Christian. No one but a Christian can pray. No one but a Christian may judge of doctrine. These make the priestly and royal office.[12]

Now, of course, Luther does not argue for anarchy or suggest that just anyone in the Church can perform these functions, although in principle, there is nothing to stop this happening. He has a strong doctrine of calling or vocation, whereby the Church calls and sets apart certain people to perform these roles on behalf of the others. However, the consequence of his argument is the radical step of questioning the practice of calling ministers in the Church 'priests'. He doesn't ban it outright, but raises serious objections to its use, arguing that it is misleading, as it arrogates what is the function of all Christians to just a few, thus emasculating the Church, and eroding the sense of the Church as a community of people ministering the promise and goodness of God to one another and the world:

> On this account I think it follows that we neither can nor ought to give the name priest to those who are in charge of Word and sacrament among the people. The reason they have been called priests is either because of the custom of heathen people or as a vestige of the Jewish nation. The result is greatly injurious to the church. According to the New Testament Scriptures better names would be ministers, deacons, bishops, stewards, presbyters.[13]

Here is a classic Reformation argument about priesthood. It does not deny the idea, nor remove it from the Church in the name of the overall doctrine of the priesthood of Christ, but extends it to all Christians.

An important observation needs to be made at this point. As Timothy Wengert points out, the phrase 'the priesthood of all believers' is never used by Luther or in fact any of the sixteenth-century Reformers, but was first used in nineteenth-century German Pietistic circles.[14] The move that Luther makes is not so much to apply the idea of priesthood to the laity, but effectively to deny the distinction between the laity and the clergy altogether. There is for him only one Christian status, or '*Stand*' (to use the German word), that is, baptized Christians serving in different offices in the Church. Luther denies the classic medieval distinction between the spiritual (clerical) and temporal (lay) estate. He replaces them both with one single Christian estate: in effect, there is no such thing as the laity. He doesn't, of course, mean that anyone can preach, or perform clerical functions, but rather that all are called to serve one another, in different ways and offices. Some are called to act as pastors or priests, others as magistrates, others as teachers and so on. For Luther it is baptism that stands as the common way into the Christian life. Christians never 'possess' an office, rather they 'hold' it, temporarily, as it were. Luther denies the idea of indelible orders, arguing that a Christian might take up or lay down these different functions at different times. There is in the Christian Church 'a single walk of life, but many offices'.[15] Every Christian serves his or her fellow Christians, either by making shoes, cleaning away rubbish, preaching in church or presiding at the Eucharist. While Pietism tends to have the laity holding sway over the clergy, and the Catholic tendency is to have the clergy holding sway over the laity, Luther abolishes the distinction altogether.[16]

Calvin on priesthood

John Calvin develops a similar critique of medieval priesthood, based on the same fundamental premises, but leading in a different direction. In the Catechism of the Church in Geneva of 1546, Calvin defines priesthood in these terms: 'It is the office and prerogative of presenting oneself before the face of God to obtain grace, and of offering sacrifice, which may be acceptable to him, to appease his wrath.'[17] The definition could, of course, have been accepted by one of Calvin's Catholic opponents, as a description of sacerdotal priesthood, but Calvin's intent is to argue that if this is what a priest really is, then there is only one priest, Christ himself.

In his *Institutes*, Calvin uses this notion of the unique priest-hood of Christ to criticize the exclusivity of the idea of papal primacy. He opposes the argument that just as the Jews had a high priest, so the Church needs a pope, on a number of grounds, not least the decree of the Council of Carthage in AD 256 that proclaimed: 'Let none be called prince of priests or first bishop.'[18] For Calvin, the key argument, however, is that the Old Testament priesthood has been transferred to and fulfilled in Christ:

> No one is ignorant of the fact that the high priest was a type of Christ; with the priesthood transferred, the right should be trans-ferred [Hebrews 7.12]. But to whom was it transferred? Obviously, not to the pope (as he dare shamelessly boast) when he takes the title unto himself, but to Christ, who, as he alone keeps that office without vicar or successor, consequently resigns that honour to no one else.[19]

In the same manner, Calvin develops a critique of exclusive ideas of ministerial priesthood. In 1540, he published a *Treatise on the Lord's Supper*, mainly to mediate between the Lutheran and Reformed parties on the question of the interpretation of the Eucharist that was raging at the time. In the course of the work, he mounts a stinging critique of the idea of the sacrament as sacrifice, and hence the idea of ministers as sacrificial priests. The Lord's Supper is not a sacrifice because there is only one sacrifice for sins – the one offered by Christ in his body on the cross. Language of the mass as 'applying to us the virtue of his intercession' is misleading, as the benefits of his sacrifice are only received by believing the word, confirmed in the sacrament, that offers us God's grace in Christ. The direction of the mass for Calvin is not upwards, as if we offer a sacrifice to God for our sins, but downwards, in that God offers us grace:

> we need bring nothing of our own, to merit what we seek; we have only to receive by faith the grace which is there presented to us, which indeed does not reside in the sacrament, but points us to the cross of Christ as its source.[20]

If the mass is not a sacrifice, there is no need for a sacrificing priesthood: 'If we do not confess Jesus Christ to be the sole sacrificer, or as we commonly call it, Priest, by whose intercession we are restored to the Father's favour, we despoil him of his honour, and do him grave hurt.'[21] Calvin acknowledges (in rather disapproving terms) the Patristic use of the term 'sacrifice' for the Eucharist, but argues that this usage refers to the sacrament as 'a memorial of the unique sacrifice'.[22] He goes on to critique the idea of a sacrificial priesthood in the Church, using virtually the same language as he would use to define priesthood in his 1546 Catechism: 'Moreover, the office of Jesus Christ has been attributed to those who are called priests, that is, persons sacrificing to God, and by sacrificing interceding for us, and so obtaining grace and pardon for our faults.'[23]

For Calvin, as for Luther, the word 'priest' is appropriate, not for a special caste within the Church, but for all Christians. Rather than focusing on the idea of mutual ministry, which is what Luther finds in the priesthood of the Church, Calvin has in mind the way in which all Christians are, like Christ, called to offer themselves to God in worship and sacrifice: 'In him we are all priests, but to offer praises and thanksgiving, in short, to offer ourselves and ours to God.'[24] Priestliness is indeed about offering a sacrifice, but this is the sacrifice of worship, offered to God from the heart.

Calvin's argument against the medieval notion of priesthood is not so much that it detracts from the priesthood of the Church, as Luther had argued, but that it detracts from the priesthood of Christ. Both Reformers mount a critique of medieval views of priesthood on similar grounds – that true priesthood belongs first to Christ and second to the Church. Yet the direction of their arguments are different. Luther's primary critique of medieval priesthood was that it had been wrested from the whole Church, because it truly belongs to all Christians. Calvin's critique was that it had been wrested from Christ, because it truly belongs to him.

Now these critiques are theologically grounded, well worked out positions, and need to be taken seriously. The argument we developed in the last chapter, drawn from the letter to the Hebrews, might also be taken to lead in the same direction. It holds tightly to the centrality and uniqueness of Christ's mediation, as we saw in the last two chapters, as well as seeing clearly the extension of the notion of priesthood in the New Testament to the Church itself. The basic fact is that the New Testament does only speak of two main types of priesthood: the priesthood of Christ and the priestly character and calling of the Church. There is no mention of the word *hiereus* in relation to Christian ministers – a whole range of other words are used (*presbuteros, episkopos, diakonos, apostolos,* etc.), but not *hiereus*.

Christ's priesthood and ours

Where then does the argument lead from here? The beginnings of an answer can be found in distinguishing Luther's own critique of priesthood from the later Protestant idea of the 'priesthood of all believers'. Very often in later Protestantism, especially in Pietistic forms of it, the 'priesthood of all believers' effectively meant the removal of any human mediator between the individual Christian and God. This was often an understandable reaction to excessive clerical domination, requiring a specific person with ecclesiastical status to mediate an individual Christian's relationship to God. The Pietistic version of the priesthood of all believers grew out of an egalitarian spirit, an instinct that no Christian stands any higher than any other.[25] In this way of thinking, I am my own priest, able to communicate directly with God, with no need for any other Christian to mediate. It can lead to a solitary individualism, a conviction that the essence of Christian faith is a personal relationship with God, with the Church as a secondary, and rather optional, extra. In this analysis, the Reformation critique of priesthood is taken to mean direct access to God through Christ, not needing any other mediator, not even my fellow Christians or the Church. In this view, personal faith is primary, and corporate Christian existence is secondary. The Church fades into the background as an ancillary aid to faith, rather than something central to the purposes of God.

Speaking strictly, however, as we have seen, Luther and the other Reformers do not so much teach the priesthood of all believers as the priesthood of the whole Church. The two ideas are subtly, yet importantly, different. In fact, Luther's understanding of the priesthood of Christians means the opposite of the usual individualistic idea of the priesthood of all believers. It emphatically does not mean that I have no need of my fellow Christian. Instead, it means that I am a priest to my fellow Christians, just as they are to me. As William Lazareth puts it: 'we are not our own priests, but our neighbours' priests, for the biblical Church is essentially a baptized priesthood that also has an ordained ministry'.[26] The Pietistic version of the idea effectively deletes the idea of priesthood, saying that all Christians are laity.

Luther's understanding is the exact opposite – that all Christians are priests. We all have an active responsibility to each other and need each other. I need the Church. I need my fellow Christians to mediate Christ to me. As Luther put it in one of his Christmas Day sermons, 'he who wants to find Christ, must first find the Church'.[27] All the seven functions of priesthood which Luther listed are vital for any healthy Christian life – without them, Christian life cannot be sustained, and every Christian needs their fellow Christians to help them live such a healthy Christian life. This is part of Luther's basic doctrine of Creation, where he sees the physical created order as a means by which we access God – it is God's mask (*larva*), which both reveals and conceals God at the same time. For Luther, God's approach to us is always indirect, not direct, through created things, not apart from them. As he says in the course of the eucharistic debates with the Swiss Reformers: 'The Spirit cannot be with us except in material and physical things such as the Word, water and Christ's body and in his saints on earth.'[28] Christ is mediated to us through each other, in the priestly calling of each Christian towards his or her fellow Christian. For Luther the doctrine of the priesthood of the Church is about the priesthood of individual Christians, but not in a sense that makes them independent of each other, but radically *inter*dependent.

Interdependence

Now this sense of interdependence perhaps gives us the clue to the way in which the priesthood of Christ plays out in the rest of the divine economy. The doctrine of Christ's priesthood tells us that we do not access God directly, but we approach him only through Christ. It is only by being in Christ that we can participate in God, be reconciled to him, and finally reach our true destiny in him. It establishes our basic *dependence* on Christ, and tells us in the most radical way possible, that we cannot approach God alone – we are incapable of finding our true selves, our final fulfilment by ourselves. Yet this radical dependence on Christ is expressed in our interdependence with one another in the Church, which is the body of Christ. We can no more make it without each other than we can make it without Christ, precisely because, at least according to Luther, Christ comes to us in our neighbour and fellow Christian, and our neighbour and fellow Christian are themselves in Christ. The doctrine of the priestly character of Christ establishes our basic *dependence* on him, as the only one through whom we have access to the Father. The doctrine of the priestly character of the Church establishes our basic *interdependence* on each other. We are incapable of being sustained in Christian life alone. In both cases, the doctrine of priesthood stands over against *independence*.

The idea of priesthood therefore contradicts the kind of spirituality that emphasizes my own personal spiritual journey to God, the solitary, lonely path, ascending upwards to the heights of awareness through isolated meditation, or some other spiritual exercises, which require neither Christ nor other people. This kind of spirituality is exactly what would be expected in a deeply individualistic culture which values privacy, independence and consumer choice; in other words, the kind of culture that surrounds us in the increasingly globalized atmosphere of the contemporary world. The kind of spirituality where the consumer is king is bound to lead to atomized, bespoke pathways to God, where the spiritual life is akin to choosing one's own customized route to God, my own personalized version of mystical advancement.

The doctrine of the mediatory priesthood of Christ establishes once and for all that there is no direct access to God in that way. The gulf between Creator and Creation, especially fallen Creation, is just too wide. As Emil Brunner puts it: 'the gulf that yawns between the creature and the Creator is deep and vast', and can only be bridged by a mediator who does not merely point to a revelation independent of himself, but is that very revelation.[29] Once that principle of a radical dependence on Christ as our Mediator with God is in place, we can see that that sense of dependence stretches into a radical interdependence on each other within the Church. And it is complete interdependence. This vision of the Church involves not the dependence of some on others, but of all on all. Everyone has something to give, something to offer, and each needs every other part of the Church. St Paul's vision of the Church as a body, with each part dependent on the other, chimes with this idea of priesthood. Paul sees the Church as the body of Christ – made up of various parts which all need one another to truly be the body of Christ:

> The eye cannot say to the hand, 'I don't need you!' And the head cannot say to the feet, 'I don't need you!' On the contrary, those parts of the body that seem to be weaker are indispensable, and the parts that we think are less honourable we treat with special honour. (1 Cor. 12.21–23)

Christians are not priestly in their individual relationship with God but in their relationships with each other. By its very interdependence, the Church is the body of Christ on earth.

So far we have begun to explore how Luther's doctrine of priesthood establishes a clear link between Christ's priesthood and that of the Church. At the same time, Calvin's theology of priesthood can also paradoxically be used to see Christ's priesthood working in other aspects of the divine economy.

Participation

One theme in Calvin's theology that has emerged with greater clarity in recent years is his doctrine of Christians' participation in Christ.[30] Todd Billings has pointed out how Calvin holds together the idea of God's forensic pardon with the idea of a true participation of the believer with God. For Calvin, the union of humanity and divinity in Christ becomes possible for believers as well in their adoption through the Spirit. The Spirit is the one who unites us with Christ so that we know the love of the Father, and intimate participation in God.[31] While keeping the firm distinction between the Creator and the creature, Calvin argues that the believer does 'enjoy true participation in Christ'.[32]

Julie Canlis points out Calvin's emphasis on our participation, not so much directly in God, but rather in Christ, with the goal of communion with God through him. It is only in Christ the Mediator that we can relate to God, yet this union in Christ through the Spirit is one that brings a deeply intimate communion with him.[33] Calvin distinguishes between the creature and the Creator in order to relate them properly and intimately. For Calvin, the divine and the human do not fuse. For him, the human ascent to God is 'into sonship, but never as The Son'.[34] Participation in God is not dissolving ourselves into God but finding ourselves in God.

Now this idea of participation in Christ opens the door to seeing how we also might participate in his priesthood. If we are able to participate in Christ by the Spirit, then it is in principle possible to participate in his priesthood. Christ is the unique Son, yet by the Spirit we can share in Sonship. In the same way, Christ is the unique Priest, yet by the Spirit we can share in his priesthood.

This idea opens up the possibility of human participation in the priestly work of Christ.

There is a vital distinction to be made here, however. Christ is the Son of God by nature. We become sons and daughters of God by grace. We are children of God because he is the true Son of God and we share in that privilege by virtue of being incorporated into Christ, united with him by the Holy Spirit. He remains the only Son of God. We do not have a kind of 'parallel' sonship which is like his, but instead can call ourselves children of God because 'God sent the Spirit of his Son into our hearts, the Spirit who calls out, '*Abba*, Father' (Gal. 4.6). We simply participate in his Sonship.

In the same way, Christ remains the only true High Priest. We do not have any priesthood that is outside of his. Any other priesthood held by the Church, humanity or Christian ministers is a sharing in Christ's priesthood, a way in which his priesthood is exercised within the world. Calvin himself makes exactly this point: 'Christ plays the priestly role, not only to render the Father favourable and propitious toward us by an eternal law of reconciliation, but also to receive us as his companions in this great office.'[35] In other words, all that Christians do in the name of Christ, Christ does through them. We are invited to participate in the priestly work of Christ as the 'everlasting intercessor'. Christ is the one who sacrifices for the sins of the world, who blesses, sanctifies, absolves and makes an offering of human life to the Father. The Church does not participate in the work of Christ by 'doing its own thing', proceeding with its own agenda separate from Christ, but by being the agent of Christ's priestly work within the world.

This chapter has explored the Reformation 'critique' of priesthood, and found it to be not so much a critique of the idea of priesthood as a protest against its restriction to a certain group of people within the Church. The Reformers stressed the priestly character of the Church perhaps more than any other movement in Christian history. Christ is the only true High Priest. Yet at the same time, the Church can be called priestly because Christ's priestly ministry, that of mediating God's presence to us and perfecting us in holiness, is carried out precisely through the Church. It is in the Church, in the relationships between Christian people, that the means of grace are mediated. It is from other Christians that we receive baptism, the word of grace, bread and wine, absolution, love and prayer – in other words, Christ is mediated to us through each other, not directly. It is not so much that Christ's priesthood is extended into the Church, as if the Church had its own priesthood separate or parallel to that of Christ, but rather that the Church participates in Christ's priesthood, and is the channel through which it operates.

Now this is a vital principle in what follows. If the Church can be said to participate in the unique priesthood of Christ, then it opens up the question of how this works in the broader canvas of the divine economy. We saw, at the end of the last chapter, the way in which the letter to the Hebrews glimpses the new heavens and the new earth. The following chapters begin to explore how this pattern of priesthood of Christ works, and how his priestly work is carried out within the world.

4

The priesthood of humanity

———•◦•◦•———

The last chapter explored the Reformation analysis of priesthood, concluding that far from it being a movement that rejected priesthood, in fact it made it a major category for understanding the person and work of Christ and the nature of the Church. At the same time, Reformation thinkers did mount a theologically rigorous critique of the practice of limiting priesthood to just a few people in the Church. It argued for a more egalitarian type of ecclesiology, based on dependence on Christ as the one true priestly Mediator between God and humanity, and interdependence on one another in the mutual priesthood of the Church, which is the agent of Christ's priestly work in the world.

We also began to explore the precise ways in which Christ's priesthood works in the Church. For Luther, this was due to Christians mediating Christ to each other through the priestly ministry of the word, prayer, preaching, sacrament and so on. For Calvin, it is in the idea of participation in Christ. This all reflects, of course, the New Testament language we explored earlier, that envisages Christ's priesthood exercised through his body, the Church, this 'kingdom of priests'. If the principle is established that Christ's priestly work of mediation and perfecting is carried out through the Church, then might this same pattern be seen elsewhere in Scripture? Might it be that this idea of priesthood is somehow central to the relationship between God and his Creation?

As we saw in Chapter 2, we can summarize the character of priesthood, as revealed by Christ, the archetypal and true High Priest, in three primary ways.

1 *Mediating*: Christ is the true High Priest precisely because he shares both in human and divine nature – he is a mediator, not an intermediary. The priesthood of Christ involves mediating between God and the world, overcoming the difference between God and Creation by uniting both. As the Mediator he intercedes for us at the right hand of the Father.

2 *Perfecting*: Christ's priesthood consists in his perfecting work: Christ as priest, through the Spirit, perfects Creation, taking on created human flesh, enabling it to become all that it was intended to be. As such he brings the divine blessing to bear upon the world, without which it cannot become what it is intended to be.

3 *Offering*: Christ as the priest offers up a perfect human life as a sacrifice to the Father, as an act of worship. Christ therefore is the true worshipper in whom all our worship is directed to the Father.

Can we see this pattern of mediating, perfecting and offering, of interceding, blessing and worshipping elsewhere in the Scriptures? The following chapters trace how Christ's priestly, mediatorial work is played out in various aspects of the way in which God relates to the world.

Created for joy

The Creation accounts in the book of Genesis do not tell us why God created the heavens and the earth. They just tell us that he did. To find the beginnings of a reason, we need to look elsewhere, to one of the other Old Testament books that develops a theology of Creation: the book of Psalms. There, Creation exists as a reflection and expression of the goodness and glory of God himself. Psalm 19 begins with the classic statement of this idea: 'The heavens declare the glory of God' (Ps. 19.1). Psalm 104 is perhaps the greatest Creation psalm in the collection, and here Creation is simply depicted as an act of joy. The poem is a litany of overflowing goodness, fruitfulness and creativity, which climaxes in verses 31–34 with this:

> May the glory of the LORD endure for ever;
>> may the LORD rejoice in his works –
> he who looks at the earth, and it trembles,
>> who touches the mountains, and they smoke.
> I will sing to the LORD all my life;
>> I will sing praise to my God as long as I live.
> May my meditation be pleasing to him,
>> as I rejoice in the LORD.

Creation is made so that in it the glory of God can be seen and 'endure for ever', but even more, that God can 'rejoice in his works'. The picture painted here is not particularly serious or earnest. Creation does not have to exist: it is contingent rather than necessary. And yet it does exist, simply because God wanted it to, as a cause for and source of joy and praise. Yet this image of God rejoicing over his Creation is only half the picture. Joy is not just the property of God, but of Creation itself, in a kind of virtuous circle of enjoyment. This joy requires not just the act of Creation, but involves a dynamic relation between God and Creation. The earth is not an inanimate object, an inert, dead thing that is incapable of response. Instead, it is called upon to reflect back to God its own joy in being created. Psalm 148, for example, depicts the entire Creation in unison, praising God without words, just by existing: 'Let them praise the name of the LORD, for at his command they were created' (v. 5). As Richard Bauckham puts it: 'all creatures bring glory to God simply by being themselves, and by fulfilling their God-given roles in God's Creation'.[1] Psalm 96 similarly depicts Creation itself praising God, but here the same note is sounded: that of sheer unadulterated joy:

> Let the heavens rejoice, let the earth be glad;
>> let the sea resound, and all that is in it.
> Let the fields be jubilant, and everything in them;
>> let all the trees of the forest sing for joy.
> Let all creation rejoice before the LORD.
>
> (Ps. 96.11–13)

Creation exists for no other purpose than joy. It is not a means to an end, an instrument through which God can fulfil certain tasks, or even an accidental by-product of conflict among the gods, as the ancient Babylonian story of *Enuma Elish* imagined it. The world exists to elicit joy, both from God and from within itself, directed back to God in praise. As Genesis puts it, the climax of Creation is when God sits back, looks at what he has made, and declares it 'very good' (Gen. 1.31).[2]

Mediating

What then, of the place of humanity? The particular character and calling of the human race emerges when we consider the early chapters of Genesis, which, as most commentators suggest, offer us two accounts of the Creation placed side by side. The first Creation account, in 1.1—2.3, emphasizes the link between humanity and God. The crucial section is this:

> Then God said, 'Let us make mankind in our image, in our like-ness, so that they may rule over the fish in the sea and the birds in the sky, over the livestock and all the wild animals, and over all the creatures that move along the ground.' So God created mankind in his own image, in the image of God he created them; male and female he created them. God blessed them and said to them, 'Be fruitful and increase in number; fill the earth and subdue it. Rule over the fish in the sea and the birds in the sky and over every living creature that moves on the ground.' (1.26–28)

Humanity is created as a reflection of God within Creation, not in the likeness of anything on earth, but of God himself. Humanity's role within Creation is to 'rule'. In other words, humanity exercises a kind of delegated divine authority. That includes the task of 'filling the earth'. Recalling the picture of overflowing fecundity and life in Psalm 104, humanity has the role of shaping, controlling and channelling that boisterous living growth. Humanity is placed 'over' the rest of Creation, with the task of subduing the unruly growth of an abundant and fertile world, thus enabling it to be an ordered and fruitful place, supporting life and giving joy. This account connects humanity to God, implying that uniquely among created beings, humanity is related to, represents and reflects the nature or image of God within the world.

However, this is not the only Creation account in these early chapters of Genesis. In the second version, in Genesis 2.4–25, humanity is created not by some special divine fiat, direct from divine substance, but from pre-existent created matter, 'from the dust of the ground' (2.7). The human race is created out of the dirt of the earth, unquestionably part of Creation, sharing in its earthy physicality. Humans come into being in exactly the same way as the animals, who are also 'formed out of the ground' (2.19). When Eve is created, she is also made out of already-formed bodily matter – out of the rib of Adam. The picture here is that of humanity emerging out of the dust, with its feet firmly on the earth, made of the same stuff as the rest of Creation, sharing the nature of both the animate and inanimate Creation. Here, there is no talk of the divine image, but instead of a special calling, which we will discuss in a moment.

In other words, the inclusion of these two accounts side by side in the same final version of the text make the point that humanity relates closely both to God and Creation. The first Creation account emphasizes the connection between humanity and divinity; the second emphasizes the connection between humanity and the earth. The primary reality is that we are created beings, part of Creation, as the second account states more categorically. We are not God. And yet, we are at the same time set apart within that Creation, alone among the animals, to bear the divine image and likeness.

As we have seen, Christ's priestly identity consists in his sharing the nature of both God and humanity. In the human identity and calling outlined here in Genesis we see an echo of that same pattern.

As we saw in the last chapter, we are sons and priests only because we share in the Sonship and priesthood of Christ, not because we have any sonship or priesthood separate from or parallel to his. In Romans 5 as well as 1 Corinthians 15, Paul makes the explicit link between Adam and Christ. Adam is 'a pattern of the one to come' (Rom. 5.14). Christ is the last Adam (*eschatos Adam*), the perfected human, the one who does what Adam was called to do – to exercise responsible and loving mastery over Creation in a way that enhances and develops rather than destroys it. It is in this light that Jesus' nature miracles are best seen. When Jesus stills storms, multiplies scraps of bread into food to feed thousands, heals broken bodies and walks on the surface of the sea of Galilee, he is doing what Adam was called to do – to rule over the inanimate Creation, to enable it to reach its potential to supply the needs of all living things, to find full restoration from the ravages of fallenness, to support rather than destroy life. Jesus is the last, the second Adam, sharing the divine nature by nature not grace.

A distinction made by many Patristic theologians may help to grasp this. Basil the Great, for example, suggests that humans are made in the *image* of God, but have to grow into his *likeness*.[3] In this sense all human beings are created in the image of God. However, in Christ we see a human being fully displaying not just the image but also the *likeness* of God, because he shares fully in the divine nature, by which alone we can come to share God's likeness.

The key point, however, is that the human race on the one hand is an emphatic part of Creation, not exalted above it, made of the dust of the ground. Yet at the same time it is summoned out of that very Creation to bear the divine image and represent God within the world. If Christ is the priest of Creation, mediating between God and the world as the divine–human Son of God, then his priestly work of mediating the love of God to the world and perfecting it is carried out first and foremost through the human race itself.

Created and called

Humanity is emphatically not God. We are part of Creation. Yet while being made from the dust of the earth, Adam also bears the divine likeness. While humanity clearly shares in created matter, we share in the divine *image*, rather than the divine *nature*. Humanity is definitely *created*, but we stand out from that Creation by being specifically *called* out from it to play a distinct role in and towards it. Humanity is called out of the rest of Creation to bear the divine image, in order that the divine blessing which is given in Christ might extend to the rest of Creation, and that Creation might be offered up to God in worship.

If humanity stands between Creation and God, with its roots in the earth, yet forged in the image of God, what does that image consist of? Much ink has been spilt trying to specify what distinguishing feature possessed by humanity denotes the image of God. Is it the possession of an inner soul? The upward stance, looking to the heavens? The technological mastery of nature? Intelligence and the ability to think rationally? The gift of language? A capacity for love? The difficulty is that it is hard to see any of these as being entirely lacking in other animal life. We may have these in a greater degree than other animals, but it is difficult to prove any of these are entirely absent in what are especially our closest cousins in the animal world. This, of course, is exactly what we should expect if human beings are made from the same material as the animals, sharing with them in the fellowship of created beings.

Instead, perhaps we should think of the image of God as primarily to be found, not so much in the idea of humanity's abilities, but in this sense of its distinct calling. Humans differ from other animals not in the possession of some distinct quality that other animals do not have, but rather in that they are called to a specific role and task within Creation. It is not so much that humans possess certain abilities that qualify them to carry the image of God. It is perhaps more the other way round: it is because humans are uniquely called out of all the other species of animal on the planet to bear the image of God, that we have developed the qualities needed to fulfil that calling within the world.

So what is that calling? We see the human vocation first in God's placing the man and the woman, these joint image-bearers of God, in the Garden of Eden, 'to work it and take care of it' (Gen. 2.15). Here are two distinct roles: that of nurture and protection. Humanity is chosen out of all the species of animals on the earth to 'work' the earth, to develop it, to enable it to reach its full potential, to make it fruitful and productive of food to nourish the animate Creation, to enable it to produce joy. At the same time, there is the call to 'take care of it', to protect it from harm, to restrain the forces that would dismantle it, destroy it and suck it back into the chaos and nothingness from which it came. According to this seminal biblical account, nurture and protection of the whole created order are therefore at the very heart of the human vocation – it is what we are here for.

This is a vision of the world that gives a special, particular role to humanity, yet is not at all anthropocentric. On this account, the world is not made for humanity; rather it is the other way round: humanity is made to care for and nurture the rest of Creation. And Creation exists not for the sake of humankind, but for the glory of God – for the joy of both.

But how is this calling fulfilled? Four areas suggest themselves, each of them having a priestly character: perfecting, or nurturing, Creation; caring for and protecting it; offering it back to God in worship; and thanksgiving.

Perfecting

As we have seen, the priestly calling is to bring Creation to full maturity, to 'perfect' it. The first aspect of this calling on humanity is the vocation to 'work' Creation (Gen. 2.15). One of the initial ways in which this plays out is in the calling to name the animals

(Gen. 2.19–20). After describing the creation of the animals, the text says that God 'brought them to the man to see what he would name them; and whatever the man called each living creature, that was its name'. Humanity is invited to use the precious gift of language to bring order to Creation, to describe it, to give each animal individuality and identity. Without a name, the 'wild animals and the birds of the sky' are simply a faceless part of the whole mass of created matter. With a name, each one is given the dignity of difference, its uniqueness identified by the diverse names given to each one by its human counterparts.

In these intriguing, brief but rich images that outline the human calling within Creation, so much comes into view. The task of naming the animals suggests the whole of the scientific endeavour to explore, understand and identify the various elements of the world and how they function. At the same time, the use of language to give order and meaning also hints at poetry and literature, the crafting of language to describe the world, the interaction of humanity with its environment, and human experience itself. There is a playfulness about the picture of God bringing the animals to the man to 'see what he would name them'. God sits back to watch this interaction between humanity and the animals. He gives genuine freedom and responsibility to the man, neither doing the naming himself, nor determining the man's choice of names. The man is entirely free to name them as he wishes – and whatever name he chooses, sticks.

The call to 'work' the earth implies technology – the attempt to take the earth's materials and minerals and re-craft them into items of housing, shelter, tools, machines and furniture. It also hints at the visual arts, with the shaping of stone or bronze into sculpture, or the mixing of the earth's pigments into paint to create images depicting and interpreting the world in graphic form.

In other words, the whole of Creation is meant to be and become more itself through the human presence in its midst. It is intended as a source of joy and rejoicing both by God its Creator, and within itself. And humanity is given a vital role in enabling that to happen, in enabling Creation to be fruitful, to sustain life, to be ordered and shaped into patterns that demonstrate God's goodness, to receive the divine blessing. As Colin Gunton puts it:

> To image the being of God towards the world, to be the priest of creation, is to behave towards the world in all its aspects, of work and of play, in such a way that it may come to be what it was created to be, that which praises its maker by becoming perfect in its own way.[4]

In theological terms, this perhaps explains the remarkable evolution of the human species in a way that outstrips any other in creativity, technological ability and language. These are precisely the qualities needed to nurture and develop Creation, in obedience to the divine calling. The tragedy is that they are also the very qualities that enable humanity to destroy the planet and each other.

Creation care

Alongside the calling to work Creation, there is also the vocation to 'take care' of it (Gen. 2.15). This is the calling to nurture and to protect the earth, or to 'rule over it' in God's name, so that it can reach its true potential. God's care for the world is expressed through the human calling to nurture, protect and describe it, to develop it and to guard it from destructive danger, to enable it to be a place and source of joy, for both God and its inhabitants. The call to take care of the earth indicates the whole movement of ecological concern, Creation care and the urge to prevent damage created by earthquakes, tsunamis, fire or even those forces that are more likely to destroy the earth in the longer term – human pollution of the atmosphere, destruction of the rainforests, elimination of species through over-hunting, or the poisoning of life in the rivers or seas.

Creation comes out of nothing. Yet always at the fringes of the story there is the possibility that Creation will be undone, unravelled, and return to the chaos out of which it came. This is the alluring but dreadful possibility that is presented before Adam and Eve in the Garden in the story of the snake, tempting them with knowledge, not just of good, but also of evil. Little do they know that this apparently tiny act of disobedience, the transgression of the divine limits set around them, placing themselves at the centre of the universe rather than God, will in fact unleash a havoc of destruction that threatens to undo all the goodness of all that exists. On this understanding, evil is sheer destructiveness. It is not at all creative, it simply undoes Creation. This plays out in our own day in the damage and destruction we have wreaked in recent centuries on the planet itself through our destruction of forests, ozone layers and pure seas. The tragedy is that human beings, the very part of God's Creation called to prevent its descent into chaos, are the very ones bringing about its destruction.

What this says, however, is that Creation care and ecological concern is not primarily a Christian calling, but a deeply human one. It is not just Christians who are called to care for the environment, but all human beings. It is good that there are a number of Christian organizations that focus on ecological concern, but they must always remember this is not ultimately a burden for Christians – it lies at the door of all people, the entire human race. Through protecting Creation from harm, humanity helps bring the divine blessing, the movement of Creation towards its renewal and fulfilment.

Offering

There is a further element to the priestly role of humanity in Creation, however. So far, we have focused on the role of humanity to represent God within Creation, to be his agents, as it were, bringing order, meaning and protection to it. Yet humanity is also called to another role: not just to represent God before Creation, but to represent Creation before God. And this happens in two primary ways.

First, in Genesis 4, we find the story of Cain and Abel, which offers the first depiction of worship in the Bible. Here, the two brothers bring offerings to God, Cain offering 'the fruits of the soil' (4.3) and Abel offering 'fat portions from some of the firstborn of his flock', representing the inanimate and animate Creation together (4.4). Of course, the rest of the story recounts how God accepts Abel's offering and rejects Cain's. However, the main point to note in this context is the way the text describes worship – it is the offering of Creation back to God.

Some parts of the Church interpret this as the essential focus of worship. This is the action reproduced in the Eucharist, the taking of bread and wine, the 'fruit of human hands' which is then offered back to God in worship.[5] Worship has always involved some element of sacrifice, so that what we do in worship is to offer back to God what he has already given us, yet transformed by human activity from grain and grapes to bread and wine. In this way, the human calling is to offer back to God the Creation itself. Other parts of the Church are wary of linking the offering of Creation back to God to the Eucharist, in the light of the self-offering of Christ, once and for all, as the true act of human worship to God.[6] The fear is that this will confuse our offering to God with Christ's offering himself as the one true offering for sin. Our offerings to God are our worship to him, they do not atone for our sins.

Either way, the primary act of worship in the New Testament is the offering of our own human bodies themselves, these physical created things, as living sacrifices, as an act of spiritual worship (Rom. 12.1), as an echo of and response to the offering of Christ's body on the cross. As it says in Hebrews, 'Christ . . . as high priest of the good things that are now already here . . . through the eternal Spirit offered himself unblemished to God' (9.11–14), or in Ephesians, 'Christ loved us and gave himself up for us as a fragrant offering and sacrifice to God' (5.2).

In Romans 12, this self-offering of our bodies, this living sacrifice, plays out in serving, giving, governing, blessing, etc. (Rom.

12.6–14). Money can be transformed from filthy lucre into 'a fragrant offering, an acceptable sacrifice, pleasing to God',[7] when it is given as a gift in the name of Christ. Cain and Abel offer the fruit of their labour, Cain offering the food he has grown and Abel offering the best of the livestock he has reared. Offering the fruit of work back to God becomes an act of worship.

All of this activity is an act of fulfilment of and obedience to the divine mandate to protect and nurture the life of the world, to build a functioning human society. An act of generosity, giving a gift to the poor or an act of service which devotes time to a friend becomes a means of offering created things such as money, possessions and time not only to the neighbour, but also to God. In this way each of these can become forms of worship. Of course, all this can be done without reference to God, solely for human pride or vanity, but when work becomes directed towards God, done for his sake, it becomes an act of worship. Colossians 3.23–24 says:

> Whatever you do, work at it with all your heart, as working for the Lord, not for human masters [lit. 'not for men'], since you know that you will receive an inheritance from the Lord as a reward. It is the Lord Christ you are serving.

The implication is clear that human work, done not for reward or out of drudgery, but performed for the sake of Christ, is a true act of service and worship offered to God.

Thanksgiving

However, there is another way in which humanity offers up Creation: we are meant to voice the silent praise of the rest of the created order. The human gift of language that we saw in Genesis 2.19 is to be used not only to name the animals, to bring order and dignity to Creation, it is also given so that one part of Creation (humanity) can offer praise on behalf of the rest of it, to express the joy of Creation. This dynamic comes to the fore in the Bible's worship manual, the Psalms. When Psalm 65.13 says, 'The meadows are covered with flocks, and the valleys are mantled with corn; they shout for joy and sing', we know that is a kind of metaphor. Of course meadows and valleys don't sing or shout. They do, however, praise God, simply by being their own created selves. Yet that praise has to come to voice. And this is the human calling: not just to praise God by work, but by words. And we do this not only on our own behalf, but on behalf of the rest of Creation. As T. F. Torrance puts it: 'Nature itself is dumb, but it is man's part to bring it to word, to be its mouth, through which the whole universe gives voice to the glory and majesty of the living God.'[8]

When humans of whatever tradition or religion speak or sing to God in worship, giving thanks for the goodness of life and the world in which we are set, they are fulfilling a divine calling to voice the silent praise of Creation itself. And this too is a priestly act, mediating between God and Creation. Jürgen Moltmann writes:

> The human being is able – and designated – to express the praise of all created things before God. In his praise he acts as representative for the whole of creation. His thanksgiving, as it were, looses the dumb tongue of nature. It is here that the priestly dimension of his designation is to be found.[9]

This praise takes a particular form in the context of Creation: that of thanksgiving. Humanity gives thanks to God for and on behalf of all of Creation for all his goodness. The first letter of Timothy 4.4–5 is one of the most remarkable statements about Creation in the Bible: 'For everything God created is good, and nothing is to be rejected if it is received with thanksgiving, because it is consecrated by the word of God and prayer.' There could hardly be a stronger affirmation of the goodness of Creation, but even more than that, it pinpoints the human calling to thanksgiving, and its consequences. Everything created, without exception, is good. And yet it still has to sanctified, made holy. The key to the sanctifying of Creation is thanksgiving. When we say grace before a meal, for example, it is as if that act turns an ordinary piece of food into a sacred gift from God. It is said to be 'consecrated by the word of God and prayer'. Literally, the word is *hagiazetai* – made holy. It is reconnected with God as it were; thanksgiving turns an object into a gift, something ordinary into something holy.

Thanksgiving and praise both echo and fulfil the priestly work of Christ, who offers himself to God on behalf of the rest of Creation. Humans are called out of the rest of Creation to represent God in the world, and the world to God. And all this is done as an expression of the offering of Christ to the Father. Humanity's priestly calling is one part of the way in which the priestly ministry of Christ is played out in the world – how the world is reconciled to God.

The hubris of humanity

This conclusion is contested, however. Christian theologies of Creation have sometimes been criticized for an overly human-centred vision, which has led to a disastrous assumption that humanity's rule over Creation gives it a right to do as it wishes with the natural environment. If humans are allowed to rule over the planet, then that rule inevitably ends up being despotic and destructive, leading to human abuse of the natural world. Often this approach is coupled with an eschatology that assumes the destruction of the earth rather than its renewal.

According to some Christian voices, especially in the movement opposing climate change as a theory of environmental decay, if the world is going to be destroyed in a divine cataclysm, then preserving it is really a waste of time. As a result, Christian theology has often been charged with responsibility for our current ecological woes. There are many secular voices arguing that the environmental crisis can be laid fairly and squarely at the feet of the book of Genesis.[10]

Now we have already argued that this vision is far from anthropocentric. The book of Genesis actually paints a picture not of a world created for the sake of humanity, but of humanity created for the sake of the world, to enable it to be fully itself.

In the Psalms we referred to earlier, the picture is developed further. When Psalm 19 says that 'the heavens declare the glory of God; the skies proclaim the work of his hands' (v. 1), it claims that the world exists not for humanity, but for God. It is created as a reflection of the divine glory, and as an expression of divine creativity, faithfulness and love. The human calling is to nurture, protect and order Creation so that it can bring glory and joy to God its maker, and overflowing joy to Creation itself. A polluted river does not bring joy, nor does it reflect the beauty and life-sustaining energy of its Creator. The same is true of a diseased tree or a barren urban wasteland that suppresses life and colour under a concrete floor. The extinction of species diminishes the variety and abundance of the world, and limits its ability to reflect the divine richness and abundance. The tragic part of this story is that humanity has become part of the problem rather than part of the solution, damaging and diminishing the world rather than protecting and enhancing it. Yet it is clear from all this that it is a deep misunderstanding to justify from Genesis, or any other part of the Bible for that matter, human licence to abuse and use Creation simply for human productivity.

But it is not just secular voices that raise critical questions at this point. Some thoughtful Christian writers also raise questions about this idea of a human priestly role within Creation. For example, in a number of works Richard Bauckham has critiqued the whole idea of stewardship as a concept defining the relationship between humanity and Creation.[11] Bauckham sees the notion of 'stewardship' as an exhibition of hubris. Human beings are a tiny part of Creation, and simply are not capable of stewarding the earth – it effectively stewards itself. Furthermore, this idea excludes God's ongoing activity within the world, where he preserves and maintains its equilibrium through continually upholding the natural order. Most damagingly, it sets humanity over and above Creation in a vertical rather than horizontal relationship, by privileging Genesis 1 as the only account that determines the relationship between human beings and their environment. Instead, Bauckham argues that our place is not so much above Creation, but alongside it, using the earth's resources within limits. The idea of the 'image of God' means ruling 'on God's behalf' rather than 'in his place'.[12] Our rule over Creation is limited, and any sense of hierarchy over Creation is qualified by a sense of community with Creation, sharing the earth with other species, rather than just ruling over them.[13]

Bauckham makes the point we have argued above, that the picture given in the Hebrew and Christian Scriptures is not anthropocentric, or geocentric, but theocentric. It focuses not on humanity, or even the earth, but on God. Both the psalmists and Jesus in the Sermon on the Mount stress the fact that the earth provides for the needs of living creatures. We are part of Creation, along with the flowers and birds, all provided for by God.

At the same time, however, he questions whether humans should be called the priests of Creation. For him, this idea implies that Creation can only relate to God through human mediation, an argument that is refuted by the very psalms we quoted above, where Creation praises God wordlessly without any help from human intervention. Bauckham writes of the 'the anthropocentric fantasy that God relates to the rest of creation only via humans'.[14] Instead, he envisages an interdependence between humanity and Creation: Eden and Adam were made for each other, Eden to delight Adam, and Adam to cultivate Eden.[15] The idea of human priesthood over Creation is the replacement of the Platonic dualism of spirit/matter by a modern metanarrative of the technological domination of nature for human use.

Connecting Creation and Creator

Reviewing various recent Orthodox approaches to the idea of human priesthood within Creation, Elizabeth Theokritoff responds to Bauckham's critique, arguing that the idea does not necessarily imply that humanity is the only mediator between God and Creation.[16] In Orthodox theology, the priestly offering of praise by humanity does not replace the praise of the rest of Creation, but instead fulfils it. As Maximus the Confessor taught, all created things have their own '*logos*' or 'word' – a divinely given identity, which reflects the divine Word through which they were made. Humanity's praise therefore connects this inner '*logos*' of each created thing with the Word of the Creator: 'it is our specific gift to have a conscious awareness both of the creature and of the Creator whose Word it echoes, and to articulate the connection by offering up the creature's praise as our thankfulness to the Creator'.[17] It is an approach that shows how the idea of human priesthood within Creation need not lead to domination or hierarchy.

Having said that, Bauckham is right to caution against too high a place for humanity in the scheme of things. This is not least because the idea that humanity is some kind of essential mediator between God and Creation is to usurp the place of Christ, who, as the incarnate Word, is the true Mediator between God and the world. However, as we have begun to see, that priesthood is itself exercised through human agency, and while that agency is contingent, not necessary – God can do without it – he still chooses to exercise part of his rule over the world through the agency of human work and worship.

Bauckham is also right to caution against overestimating the influence of humanity over the world, and to stress its ability to survive and thrive perfectly well without human intervention. As we have seen, Genesis portrays humanity both as part of the 'community of Creation' and as set apart for a particular role within it. We belong to the earth, as we are created out of the dust, yet we also stand out, not because of any distinct ability we have, but because we alone out of all Creation have been given the responsibility to protect and nurture the rest of it.

Human impact on Creation

However, we do know from the negative elements of the human impact on the environment, that humanity can have a significant effect on Creation, to protect it or to harm it. If we are capable of destroying the planet, as our nuclear weapons and environmental recklessness suggest, then we are also capable, not so much of saving the planet, but certainly enhancing it, and in particular offering it back to God in worship and praise. The nurturing and enhancement of life on earth does require human activity. Grain does not turn into bread on its own. Chemicals do not turn into medicine spontaneously. Marble does not miraculously form itself into Michelangelo's 'David' by chance. Technology, medicine and art all enhance and protect life and Creation itself, and all are part of the human priestly calling to mediate God's love to Creation, bringing the joy which was its true purpose.

The future of Creation

A further point refers to the direction of Creation. If it comes into being through the Word, it ends in being remade in the image of Christ, the incarnate Word. The goal of the narrative of Creation in the book of Genesis is not a return to the original state, but the Sabbath rest of God. Creation moves towards a destination, which is God's future, or in the words of the letter to the Ephesians, the day when 'the times reach their fulfilment – to bring unity to all things in heaven and on earth under Christ'.[18]

It seems from the New Testament that humanity has a part to play in this. Romans 8.21–23 contains an intriguing hint:

> The creation itself will be liberated from its bondage to decay and brought into the freedom and glory of the children of God. We know that the whole creation has been groaning as in the pains of childbirth right up to the present time. Not only so, but we ourselves, who have the firstfruits of the Spirit, groan inwardly as we wait eagerly for our adoption to sonship, the redemption of our bodies.

It seems that, somehow, the future of Creation is bound up with, and in some sense waits for, the revealing of the children of God. The groaning of a fallen Creation is echoed by and echoes the groaning of suffering humanity, waiting for its re-forming into the image of Christ. Creation's destiny is to share the freedom that those who know themselves to be God's beloved children enjoy.

Christ in us, the hope of glory

The last point brings us back full circle. The idea of the priesthood of humanity can only be saved from hubris if it is seen as an expression and agent of the priestly work of Christ. Christ is the one through whom God's ongoing and life-giving love is mediated to Creation and who perfects it by his offering of himself. As we saw in Chapter 1, Christ's priesthood is eternal, before Creation itself, certainly before the creation of humanity. He is the one through whom Creation came into being and who will bring it to its completion. The human calling to nurture and care for Creation is the visible working out of this priestly work of Christ. This is how Christ does it – through humanity, which is made in his image. Humanity was elected out of Creation to do this Christ-shaped, priestly work, to be the very ones through whom God will enact 'his good pleasure, which he purposed in Christ, to be put into effect when the times reach their fulfilment – to bring unity to all things in heaven and on earth under Christ' (Eph. 1.9–10).

Humanity may be a small part of the vastness of the planet, but seen in Christ, it is a highly significant part. Humanity is called to be the agent of Christ's priestly role within Creation, developing, perfecting and protecting Creation so that it can bring the joy and blessing for which it was made, as it is offered back to God in a worshipful life.

Yet the reality we see around us is that this is far from the case. Humanity very often harms rather than helps Creation to be fully itself. Human activity is so often done for our own self-interest rather than reflecting praise back to the Creator. How then can humanity exercise its proper priestly role again, enabling Creation to become what it was always meant to be? This is where the priesthood of the Church comes into play.

5

The priesthood of the Church

The human race, despite its apparent insignificance, is called to play a vital role in making Creation joyful. Christ's priestly work, of mediating God's love to the world and enabling the world to become what it has the potential to be, is enacted through the human calling both to care for and to nurture the rest of Creation, so that it brings joy both to itself and to its Creator.

In the last chapter, we saw the common Patristic distinction between being made in the image of God and the need to grow into his likeness. Adam and Eve in the Garden are given the task of the nurture and care of Creation; however, just as for each individual human being, they have to grow in the virtue and wisdom needed to play that role fully.

Yet we all know it isn't as simple as that. That growth into maturity no longer happens in a seamless way. We humans have developed a remarkable propensity to cause pain not peace, jealousy rather than joy. The early chapters of Genesis lay out the human calling to the nurture and protection of Creation, yet they soon go on to depict in graphic terms the human tendency to refuse to play ball. The fall is a classic tale of choosing the very thing that will destroy rather than protect Creation, choosing what will undo it, rather than fulfil it. As a result, the human race, rather than being a blessing to Creation, has often become something of a curse.

In Genesis 2, immediately after the call to work and take care of Creation, Adam and Eve are told the one limit on their existence: 'You are free to eat from any tree in the garden; but you must not eat from the tree of the knowledge of good and evil, for when you eat from it you will certainly die' (v. 16–17). There is freedom to explore, to enjoy. The one experience they are warned against is the knowledge of both good and evil. Of course they know the good already, but in a sense they do not know it as 'good' because they do not know its opposite, or its absence. They simply know existence, which is good, just because it is. The knowledge of good *and evil* is the knowledge of the contrast between them, knowing good as good, precisely because they also know by experience the shadow of evil – the possibility that goodness can be threatened, or undone. So the serpent's temptation is for them to taste evil, to taste emancipation from God, making themselves 'like God' (3.5), a rival to him, separate from him. And by tasting evil, they instantly know goodness as good, but also the possibility of its opposite and absence.

Now of course this temptation to be 'like God, knowing good and evil' raises the question of whether God knows evil. And the answer is that yes he does: he 'knows' it in the sense that he knows the possibility that the goodness of Creation can be undone – it is possible that it might be destroyed, unmade. Being God, he knows what that possibility means. He knows the ugliness, the repulsiveness of it, the suffering that it will involve to a sentient Creation. He knows that is a possibility devoutly to be feared, and strenuously to be resisted.

Humans, however, do not have that wisdom. At least not yet. They are enticed, attracted by the prospect of emancipation from God. And they take and eat, not in the eucharistic spirit of receiving with thanksgiving the gift of God, but in the rebellious spirit of asserting their own independence from God, their demand of the right to knowledge, even when that knowledge is disastrous, both for them and for the whole of Creation. They do not yet know the trail of misery, pain and suffering this knowledge will bring in its train. At this stage it still seems appealing and desirable. And that is exactly the problem – their desires are at this stage immature, uncontrolled, lacking in perception or wisdom. They are made in God's image, but need to grow into his likeness. When the fruit of the tree of knowledge is eaten, a pattern of addiction sets in, and a web of behaviour settles, in which it becomes impossible to kick the habit of independence. Rather than protecting Creation, they (we) use it for their own benefit or glory and discard it when they (we) have no use for it, or when it cannot benefit them. Instead of nurturing, working with the different parts of Creation, both animate and inanimate, to draw out its potential to bring joy, they twist it and misuse it, turning ploughshares into swords, fashioning weapons from metal or words, to bring down rather than to raise up.

If the whole project of Creation is to be rescued, if it is again to become a source of joy rather than misery, humanity needs first to be saved from itself, and then turned around in order to play its true part again in the drama of history, the purposes of God. If human beings were meant to be the priests of Creation, and if they are to fulfil that divine calling, they need to be reshaped, so they can reflect the likeness of the Son through whom the world was originally created.

Of course, the story of the fall is not just contained in chapter 3 of Genesis. It runs throughout chapters 3—11, a narrative that not only depicts the seminal moment of rebellion, but the fallout in the fracturing of human community, the breakdown of the harmony between men and women (Adam and Eve), and between brothers (Cain and Abel). It continues in the fracturing of the fellowship between humans and the very earth on which they walk, in the flood which threatens to wipe out all life, where nature becomes an enemy of human life, not a friend. It even breaks the bond between humans and their own precious gift of language, the gift by which they were to name and order the world. As humans continue to assert their independence, their mastery over the world in the building of the Tower of Babel, the divine response is to limit their ability to do damage by thwarting the possibility of universal communication through the confusion of human language (11.7).

It is immediately after this that a new note strikes. Abraham is called out of obscurity, out of the far-off land of the Chaldeans, to be the father of a new community, chosen out of the rest of humanity, a priestly people. God elects Abraham and his family in response to human attempts to thwart his plan of blessing. As Christopher Seitz puts it, the election of Israel is 'the means by which sinful creation receives the blessing originally intended for it, for all nations and people'.[1]

Throughout the Old Testament, Israel, the family that continues from the line of Abraham, Isaac, Jacob, Joseph and so on, is designated as a priestly people. The first word of God to Israel after rescuing them through the exodus is to tell them precisely who they are: 'out of all nations you will be my treasured possession. Although the whole earth is mine, you will be for me a kingdom of priests and a holy nation' (Exod. 19.5–6). Even when the people go into exile, the calling to be a priestly community remains: 'you will be called priests of the LORD, you will be named ministers of our God' (Isa. 61.6).

This calling to be a priestly community develops and expands in the New Testament to include the Gentiles, and with the coming of the Spirit at Pentecost, the Church is born, as Jew and Gentile are bound together into a new people, a new community centred around Christ. As we have seen, the Church is still a priestly people, a people called to play its part in the divine drama of the priesthood of Christ. As John A. T. Robinson put it:

> In the Old Testament the priesthood . . . was to do for the people what the people as a whole could not do . . . In the New Testament the whole people of God is called to the priesthood – the priesthood of Christ. It is called to share his priesthood to the world, mediating his atoning and reconciling work.[2]

The Church is called both to enact and to direct attention to the priestly work of Christ. However, here the focus is different from the one we saw while examining the priesthood of humanity. If the human race is called to play a priestly role between God and Creation, mediating God's love to the rest of Creation, enabling it to be what it was meant to be, offering it back to God in worship, then the Church plays a priestly role specifically towards the whole of humanity, mediating God's love to the rest of the human race and enabling it to play precisely the priestly role assigned to it.

Mediating

The image of God in humanity is broken. How are people to be restored to their proper place in the divine economy, the divine pattern of mediation? How can the human race rediscover its true identity and fulfil its divine mandate?

The answer is that the Church is the agent through which Christ, through the Holy Spirit, recalls humanity to its proper place, and restores it into his own image, so that it is capable of playing its divinely ordained role within the world. As we saw in the last chapter, humanity is the one species chosen out of the whole of Creation to be God's means of blessing the rest of it, the part that enables the whole to be what it is called to be. The next link in the chain, or widening of the circle, is that the Church is the community chosen out of the whole of humanity to be God's means of blessing the whole human race. It is the part that also enables the whole to be what it is called to be and to do what it is called to do. The Church has a distinct calling not so much to the whole of Creation – that is the human calling, in which individual Christians and the Church as a whole participate by virtue of being human – but specifically to humanity. The Church's primary and priestly task within the world is mediating God's love to other people, enabling them to become what they were always intended to be and offering them as it were to God as an act of worship.

Now the Church is not the incarnate Son. It is the community in whom Christ is present and through whom he does his work in the world. Too close an identification of the Church with Christ brings dangers. The Church is fallen in a way that Christ is not. The Church does things that Christ would not do. An ecclesiology that identifies the Church as the 'continuation of the incarnation' or the ongoing presence of Christ in the world can imply that what the Church does, Christ does, so that when a priest abuses a child, that can seem like Christ abusing a child – a completely unacceptable notion. The Church is not divine. Yet just as Adam is rooted in the earth, yet is called to represent God to the rest of Creation, the Church is rooted in humanity, yet is summoned by God to represent him to all peoples.

The Church is in one sense a very human institution. The history of the Church reveals occasional moments of glorious generosity, wisdom and bold witness. Yet those also coexist alongside a great deal of unfaithfulness, betrayal and corruption. All this is not surprising, in that viewed from one angle, at least, the Church shares in the nature of any other human institution, with its structures, hierarchies and politics. The Church can be studied by social scientists and sociologists as a human construction with all the frailties and fallibilities that such bodies contain. It is made up of very ordinary people, in one sense just like all other frail and fallible people. Yet that can never be the final word about the Church. Jesus Christ is in one sense very human, with flesh and blood, emotions and needs just like any of us. Yet that can never be the final word about him – as we have seen, his identity is this unique person, both fully divine and human, sharing fully in the nature of both.

In the same way, the Church is more than a human institution. It is called by God to represent him in the world. Just as Adam is endowed with the divine image to enable him to play his unique role within humanity, the Church is endowed with the Holy Spirit, so that Spirit is present to give life and animate a passion for change and the purposes of God. It is entrusted with the message that in Christ God has not given up on his world, and continues to love it and sustain it, a message proclaimed in words, inspired by the Spirit and embodied in sacraments and the self-sacrificial love of Christ. It is described as the 'body of Christ', and while this is best seen as metaphor rather than as a literal expression,[3] it still indicates its function as the community through whom Christ enacts his priestly work among humanity.

As we saw earlier, human beings have to grow into maturity, wisdom and the likeness of God. Since the fall, that growth has become complicated, in that the addiction to self-promotion, the desire to replace and eliminate God, thinking we can do better, inhibits our ability to do the very things the last chapter described as being at the heart of the human vocation. We are no longer able, no longer inclined even, to give ourselves to the care and nurture of the world in the name of the Creator, reflecting God's nature and grace within the world, and offering it back to him in work and worship.

Something needs to happen. Each person has on the one hand to grow into his or her full potential in relation to God and others. At the same time we also need to be transformed from within, so that the desire that destroys, the urge to play God, is changed into a willingness to give ourselves to one another and to give God his due as the Creator. And that is the task of the Church.

Jesus himself points to this mediating role of the Church, between God and humanity, as his agent, doing his work:

> You are the salt of the earth. But if the salt loses its saltiness, how can it be made salty again? It is no longer good for anything, except to be thrown out and trampled underfoot. You are the light of the world. A town built on a hill cannot be hidden. Neither do people light a lamp and put it under a bowl. Instead they put it on its stand, and it gives light to everyone in the house. In the same way, let your light shine before others, that they may see your good deeds and glorify your Father in heaven. (Matt. 5.13–16)

Salt is the seasoning that draws out the true flavours or essence of the food to which it is applied. It is the part that enables the food to taste as it should. So the Church, the community of Christ, is the part of the whole that enables the rest of humanity to be as it should, that draws out its true identity. At the same time, the Church is to be the light that shines, the city that shows what cities are meant to be like. It is to shine its light into the dark corners of humanity, bringing people back to their true calling to 'glorify [their] Father in heaven'.

Just as humanity mediates between God and the world, the Church mediates between God and humanity. And each is an expression of the one unique priestly mediation of Christ, the way in which his priestly blessing is conveyed to the world so that it might again be a source of joy.

Perfecting

The Church exists as a priestly community, through which Christ is at work to enable the rest of humanity to carry out its priestly role in and towards the rest of Creation. The Church is called to no less than the perfecting of men and women, drawing them into the fellowship with God which is the only place in which that can happen, turning them from part of the problem into part of the solution, from a curse into a blessing. If Creation is to flourish, if it is to bring about the joy it was intended to bring, to God, to us and to the whole cosmos, then it requires a particular kind of person – a new humanity as it were. It needs humanity to become like Christ – capable of self-giving, sharing the divine character of love and grace, worthy to be entrusted with the power over Creation to bring in the order and healing that it needs.

Now this helps to focus the work of the Church into the area of character formation, to the healing and transformation of people. And this is where the dimension of the Church as the creation of the Holy Spirit enters the picture.

The Church began, not on Christmas Day, nor on Good Friday, nor even on Easter Day, but at Pentecost. The Church began when the Holy Spirit came to fill the people of God, to enable them to prophesy, see visions and dream dreams, so that everyone who calls on the name of the Lord can be saved (Acts 2.17–21). The early Fathers of the Church often saw the Spirit as God bringing his Creation to its fulfilment. St Basil the Great portrays the Spirit as the one who brings all things to their proper fulfilment. Angels, for example, 'exist by the will of the Father, are brought into being by the work of the Son, and are perfected by the presence of the Spirit'. With regard to all of Creation, the Father 'creates through the Son and perfects through the Spirit'.[4] So the Church as the creation of the Spirit whose particular work is this perfecting in holiness, is the place where the work of the Spirit, to draw all Creation to its eschatological future, is concentrated. And the Church is particularly focused on humanity, providing a space where people can be filled with the same Spirit, with a desire to worship, to serve, to work to the glory of God, to desire change, to see visions and dream dreams of what shape God's future might take within the world.

The Spirit does this by drawing humanity more closely into the heart of God, which is the love between the Father and the Son. Jesus Christ, the precise image and representation of God (Heb. 1.3), is the man filled with the Spirit of God, and so for people to take up again their priestly, image-bearing role within Creation requires their being filled with the same Spirit, the Spirit who makes things and people 'normal' – what they were always meant to be. The Church is therefore the space where people can be changed by their interaction with the Spirit of God and with each other.

How then does the Church play its role between God and humanity? In a number of ways hinted at in the New Testament, where we see this priestly role of the Church laid out.

Intercession

In the last chapter we noted these words in 1 Timothy:

> I urge, then, first of all, that petitions, prayers, intercession and thanksgiving be made for all people – for kings and all those in authority, that we may live peaceful and quiet lives in all godliness and holiness. This is good and pleases God our Saviour, who wants all people to be saved and to come to a knowledge of the truth.

> For there is one God and one mediator between God and mankind,
> the man Christ Jesus, who gave himself as a ransom for all people.
>
> (1 Tim. 2.1–6)

Here we find the priestly language of mediation applied to Christ.
He is the true Mediator between humankind and God, who gave
himself as a ransom to reconcile humanity to God and God to
humanity. How then is this priesthood expressed? When the Church
prays for the rest of humanity. The Church prays precisely because
Christ is the one true Mediator, and as an expression of his priestly
mediation. The Church intercedes for ordinary people, for govern-
ments and monarchs, for order, peace and dignity in human society.
It thus prays that human society will reflect the peace, dignity and
order that is God's will for human life. It also prays that people
will 'be saved and . . . come to a knowledge of the truth'. Likewise,
the Church prays for the world's governance, praying for peace
and security, for the conditions in which people can pursue godli-
ness and holiness. The Church always utters its prayer using some
such formula as: 'in Jesus' name', or 'through Christ our Lord'. This
can sometimes seem a thoughtless, routine phrase, a way of bringing a prayer to a close. However it is theologically very significant.

As we saw in Chapter 2, Christ has made the one human response
to God, in offering a perfect human life as a sacrifice for sin. The
Church therefore does not offer its own separate human response,
but instead participates in Christ's prayer to the Father. The sole
priesthood of Christ means that he continually intercedes for us
at the right hand of the Father, so that what we do when we pray
is simply to join in with his prayer – we pray in Christ. As James
B. Torrance puts it:

> By grace, we are given to participate in his intercession for all
> humanity. So in our corporate worship we are called to be a royal
> priesthood, bearing on our hearts the sorrows and cares and tragedies
> of our world, as our heavenly High Priest does.[5]

Christ intercedes (*entugchanei*) for humanity at the right
hand of the Father (Rom. 8.34); he 'always lives to intercede'

(*entugchanein* – Heb. 7.25) for us before God. So the Church also joins in, interceding for the world, offering intercessions (*entugeuxeis*). The same word is used in both Romans 8 and Hebrews 7 for Christ's work and 1 Timothy 2 for the Church's work. The Church joins in the prayer of Christ: the priestly work of Christ is carried out through the intercessory prayer of the Church.[6]

In this priestly ecclesiology, intercessory prayer becomes one of the central activities of the Church. Through the Church, Christ's mediatorial work between God and humanity is played out, enabling human society and individual people to become what they were always meant to be, first through prayer. Intercessory prayer can seem the most pointless of activities. It can seem quietist, achieving little. And this is because it relies directly on God rather than human activity for its effects. And yet it is the primary way in which Christ does his work, through the prayers of the Church, which prays for human life and lives, asking for divine action in the world to bring blessing to a world which is ravaged by injustice and pain, and at the same time, offering those lives to God in prayer.

Describing prayer as intercession highlights the way in which the person or community praying stands between those they pray for and the one they pray to. There is a representative function here, which comes into focus especially in the act of prayer. Suzanne McDonald, in a work that contrasts the theologies of Karl Barth and John Owen, develops the notion of election as representing God to others and others to God, by 'holding the non-elect other in the sphere of God's blessing', while we wait for the Parousia.[7] For her, the Church's primary calling is ontological rather than functional. The analysis perhaps needs augmenting with a more active sense in which the Church relates to the world, as we will argue in the next section of this chapter, yet the basic idea still holds. The Church stands between God and humanity in Christ, representing each to the other, holding the world before God in prayer, continually offering up a broken and hurting humanity for God's action, so that it might become again the means of divine blessing to the rest of Creation. So, the Church's prayer for healing, for example (Jas. 5.14), which has long been a central aspect of intercessory prayer,[8] is one of the chief ways in which Christ, through the Church, enables humanity to be perfected, to come to be what it has the potential to be, overcoming the effects of the fall in disease, sickness and pain. Damaged, hurting, diminished people often only limp along, consumed in their own pain, absorbed in fear of the past and the future. When instead they find themselves ransomed, healed, restored and forgiven through Christ, freed from the burden of the past through divine forgiveness, and freed from the fear of death through the promise of eternal life, then they find the energy, the motivation and desire to give themselves to each other and to the wider Creation. So, as Christ prays for the world, so the Church prays in the name of Jesus for the healing of people, not just so that they get better, or have improved health, but so they are able to play their part in the divine plan to bring joy out of Creation.

Blessing

The final act of Christ, the true High Priest, in the Gospel of Luke is to pronounce a blessing on his disciples: 'When he had led them out to the vicinity of Bethany, he lifted up his hands and blessed them. While he was blessing them, he left them and was taken up into heaven' (Luke 24.50–51). The Old Testament Levitical priesthood held the task of pronouncing divine blessing over the people of God: 'At that time the LORD set apart the tribe of Levi to carry the ark of the covenant of the LORD, to stand before the LORD to minister and to pronounce blessings in his name, as they still do today' (Deut. 10.8).

Christ's priestly blessing on the world is enacted through the Church. In the New Testament, this blessing comes especially into focus in the context of the world's rejection of the Church.

In Romans, the Church is urged to 'bless those who persecute you' (Rom. 12.14). Elsewhere Paul also describes how 'when we are cursed, we bless' (1 Cor. 4.12). The first letter of Peter 3.9 also has the same theme: 'Do not repay evil with evil or insult with insult. On the contrary, repay evil with blessing.' The Church's priestly calling is to bless the world in Christ, despite the fact that the world does not really understand it, and often rejects it.

This calling to bless is both ontological and functional. The Church is called, not just to pronounce blessing, but to be a blessing. It is to be a means, a channel of Christ's priestly blessing to people. On one level, the Church just *is* a blessing by its very presence in the world. The existence within the wider human community of a people who gather to offer worship to God, to voice the praise of Creation, to celebrate the victory which Christ has won over the powers of darkness, is itself a blessing to the world. Just by doing this, the Church acts as a visible, and sometimes audible, reminder of the ongoing commitment of God to his Creation and the simple fact that the world matters: it matters so much to God that he calls people out from the nations of that very world, to sing his praises and to celebrate his love.

Yet there is also a functional aspect to blessing. In this mode, each local church sets out to be a blessing to its local community by seeking ways to extend the grace, generosity and kindness of God to the rest of humanity in society. To be a means of channelling God's blessing to humanity means being a community that shows another way of life, another pattern of social relating than the one we are used to in regular human societies. So, for example, rather than a social life which pits people against one another, nation against nation, tribe against tribe, the Church holds out a vision that extends beyond that, of a community made up of 'every tribe and nation', where male and female, black and white, rich and poor, employer and employed meet together on the same ground, based in their common faith and baptism.

The Church also seeks to be a blessing through acts of goodness. Unlike most human communities, the Church's life focuses not on itself, but on those who do not belong. It is a community defined by its mission to be a means of blessing. A church that gets wrapped up in its own internal ordering is a church that has lost its way. It has forgotten its identity as a priestly people called to bless the world. Instead, a healthy church is one that is constantly looking for ways to bless the community around it, meeting whatever human need it is able to address out of its own resources, whether that means providing food for the hungry, shelter for the homeless, or comfort for the bereaved. The Church is most itself when it is enacting the priestly blessing of Jesus on the poor, the hungry, those who weep and those who are despised (Luke 6.20–22).

Just as humanity was given the divine charge to develop and to protect the planet (Gen. 2.15), so the Church has the same calling, to develop and protect people. The Church stands under the divine mandate to protect humanity where it can, to speak up for those who are disadvantaged, to step in where the state fails to act, to guard people from the harm that so often threatens them in a fallen and dangerous world. The Church is, at the same time, the arena in which people grow up into Christ, through the work of spiritual formation, which enables them to become disciples of Jesus. In the process, we are remade in his likeness through the Holy Spirit's sanctifying work. It is in this community that we are to be made 'perfect', becoming what we were always intended to be. The gifts of the Spirit are the means by which we minister to one another, allowing pastoral wisdom, prayers for healing, prophetic words of encouragement and Christian teaching loose in the community in a way that helps in the reconstruction of people into full perfection. The gifts of the Spirit are given to the whole Church:

> to equip his people for works of service, so that the body of Christ may be built up until we all reach unity in the faith and in the knowledge of the Son of God and become mature, attaining to the whole measure of the fullness of Christ.   (Eph. 4.12–13)

Offering

Sacrifice has always been a priestly activity. The priests in the Temple offered their daily sacrifices to God. According to the letter to the Hebrews, the sacrifices of atonement, ended by the Roman destruction of the Jerusalem Temple in AD 70, had in any case been theologically redundant for the past 40 years or so, since the death of Christ who offered himself as a sacrifice once and for all.[9] The Church does not offer itself for its own sins. As we saw in Chapter 2, Christ's self-sacrifice alone is the one necessary offering for the sins of the world. And yet the concept of offerings of worship does continue (Heb. 13.5; Rom. 1.12). While the Church does not partake in Christ's self-offering for sin, it does participate in his self-offering as worship. The language of sacrifice and offering continues to be used in the New Testament for the Church. Christians are urged to offer their bodies as 'a living sacrifice, holy and pleasing to God, this is your true and proper worship' (Rom. 12.1). The gift Paul receives from the Philippian church, delivered by the hands of Epaphroditus, most probably a financial gift, is 'an acceptable sacrifice, pleasing to God' (Phil. 4.18). The Church does continue to offer the sacrifice of praise, the sacrifice of lives, rights, ambitions given up for the sake of Christ.

This calling to bless the world is a calling that involves sacrifice, joining in his act of worship to the Father. This is no romantic calling, bringing only warmth and comfort. There is indeed a deep comfort in the gospel – the knowledge of the forgiveness of sins, the privilege of participation in the life of God – yet the proper response to that is not only security but also sacrifice. It means a willingness to pour oneself out for the sake of Christ and to become an offering to God for the sake of the people Christ came to call, the people to whom the Church is called to mediate God's love and presence.

It means the Church lives for the sake of the rest of the human race, not for the sake of its own survival. Michael Jinkins puts it like this:

The church needs to be self-forgetful, not anxious about its own survival ... The church faces death, like all of us. The church has always, throughout its history, almost routinely faced death ... The church is most attractive when it pursues its own vocation uncloncerned with its own survival.[10]

Every time a Christian gives time to help a neighbour in the name of Christ, every time a local church devotes its money and energy to setting up a food bank for the impoverished, or provides shelter for the homeless out of its own resources or buildings, it is more than a simple act of kindness – it becomes an expression of Christ's self-offering to God in thanksgiving and love, that helps draw others back into the heart of the love of God; which leads us to a further way in which the Church makes an offering to God.

Evangelism

One of the very few places in the New Testament where priestly activity is explicitly carried out by the Church or by Christians is a reference not to the Eucharist, nor even to blessing or absolution, but to evangelism. In Romans 15, Paul writes of:

... the grace God gave me to be a minister of Christ Jesus to the Gentiles. He gave me the priestly duty of proclaiming the gospel of God, so that the Gentiles might become an offering acceptable to God, sanctified by the Holy Spirit. Therefore I glory in Christ Jesus in my service to God. I will not venture to speak of anything except what Christ has accomplished through me in leading the Gentiles to obey God by what I have said and done – by the power of signs and wonders, through the power of the Spirit of God. So from Jerusalem all the way around to Illyricum, I have fully proclaimed the gospel of Christ. (15–19)

Paul's ministry of bringing the gospel to the Gentiles is seen as a priestly one. Paul is a minister (*leitourgos*) with the priestly work (*hierourgounta*) of representing God before the Gentiles by bringing the message of Christ to them. As he stands in front of Athenians,

Ephesians, Corinthians, preaching the message of grace and rescue, he speaks in the name of God, on his behalf, mediating the Word of God to them. At the same time, he sees this ministry of bringing Gentiles to know Christ as presenting them back to God as an offering (*prosphora*) acceptable to God (*euprosdektos*), sanctified (*hagiadzō*) by the Holy Spirit. The language is taken directly from the Temple in Jerusalem – it is the language we are more familiar with in the letter to the Hebrews, the language of sacrifice, of sanctified offering, of priestly work. Paul does this work as a 'minister of Christ Jesus'. He is conscious of speaking not in his own name, but in the name of Jesus Christ – God makes his appeal in the very words of Paul (2 Cor. 5.19). Here again, is Christ doing his work of offering humanity back to the Father through the evangelism of the Church. Proclaiming the gospel in the power of the Spirit is priestly work, because in it, Christ both speaks the word of God to people and offers people back to God. Paul's preaching of the gospel, accompanied by 'signs and wonders', is directed towards leading the Gentiles to 'obey God', and thus return to their true human vocation.

One of the classic texts on the priestly character of the Church comes in 1 Peter 2.9: 'you are a chosen people, a royal priesthood, a holy nation, God's special possession, that you may declare the praises of him who called you out of darkness into his wonderful light'. Here the priestly character of the Church consists precisely in its calling to sound publicly the virtues of Jesus Christ, the true High Priest. The Church is priestly when it declares the praises of Jesus Christ to people who understand neither the identity of Jesus Christ, the one through whom God blesses the world, nor their own priestly calling.

Evangelism is, perhaps surprisingly, one of the most priestly acts of the Church. Viewed in this way, it is much more than a kind of recruitment drive for church attendance or a PR campaign to increase market share. Its purpose is the praise and glory of God, or in other words, joy. In the parables recounted in Luke 15, where Jesus presents three stories, all of which refer to people being brought back into fellowship with God, being offered back to God again, the final note struck in all three is joy. When the lost sheep is found, we are told that 'there will be more rejoicing in heaven over one sinner who repents than over ninety-nine righteous people who do not need to repent' (v. 7). When the woman's coin is discovered, she says, 'Rejoice with me; I have found my lost coin.' The parable concludes, 'In the same way, I tell you, there is rejoicing in the presence of the angels of God over one sinner who repents' (v. 9–10). When the Prodigal Son returns, the last words of the Father to the elder son strike the same note: 'we had to celebrate and be glad, because this brother of yours was dead and is alive again; he was lost and is found' (v. 32). There is celebration as each of these – the lost sheep, the coin and the son – are reconciled to the one who lost them.

Christ addresses the world through the Church. The Church therefore performs its priestly activity of mediating and perfecting by making evangelism a central activity. The Church exists to pray for the world, but also to announce, to declare, to exhibit the good news of reconciliation with God, through both its words and its actions. Each person restored to fellowship with God becomes an offering to God, someone else potentially restored to play his or her own human priestly role within Creation. The church that fails to engage with this priestly activity, the church that forgets the centrality of evangelism has forgotten its true calling, to be the means whereby Christ makes his priestly offering to God of people ransomed, healed and forgiven.

Evangelism restores people to God. Through sensitive, faithful evangelism in the power of the Spirit – whatever method is used and in whatever language it is spoken – people are reconciled to God, they are opened up to God again, so that the process of transformation into the image of Christ, into the full humanity we see in him, can begin.

The priestly role of the Church therefore exists not just at its centre, in worship, prayer and sacramental activity, but also at its edges. Perhaps even primarily at its edges. Christians often feel most 'priestly', in other words, standing in a mediating position between God and the rest of humanity, when they are at work, rather than when they are in church. Being known as a Christian in the workplace, at the school gate, in local clubs or sports fields, is to represent God in a very tangible and conscious way. I well remember playing in a football team where, to my knowledge, I was the only Christian present. Other players would apologize for swearing because they were aware that I represented not only my team, but also in some sense, God himself. It is, paradoxically, one of the places where I have most felt the priestly calling to represent God to the world and to offer the world back to God in prayer and evangelism!

Worship

Besides evangelism, the other way in which the Church offers a sacrifice to God is in its worship. The author of the Hebrews urges his readers: 'Through Jesus, therefore, let us continually offer to God a sacrifice of praise – the fruit of lips that openly profess his name' (13.15). We have already seen how humanity is given the gift of language so it can voice the praises of the Creator on behalf of the rest of Creation. Yet as we know, that gift of language is used for all other kinds of speech, some of it beneficial, some of it downright damaging or hurtful, language of cursing rather than blessing. As the letter of James puts it: 'With the tongue we praise our Lord and Father, and with it we curse human beings, who have been made in God's likeness. Out of the same mouth come praise and cursing. My brothers and sisters, this should not be' (3.9–10).

As the Church mediates between God and humanity, it makes its offering of worship, looking both ways, or in two dimensions, as it were. One is that when the Church worships, it is simply joining in the worship, the self-offering of Christ. 'Worship is the gift of participating through the Spirit in the incarnate Son's communion with the Father', as James Torrance says.[11] When we worship, we simply join in Christ's worship of the Father: the Church's priestly offering of worship is never offered on its own, in parallel to or equivalent to Christ's. Instead, we are privileged to join in with the Son's fellowship with the Father.

The second dimension of the Church's worship is that it offers that worship on behalf of the rest of humanity. Humanity is not united in praise of its Creator, and so the Church is given a special calling to do that, representing the rest of the human race. Whenever the Church worships together it does so not withdrawn from, or in opposition to, the rest of humanity. The rest of the human race may not be aware of its calling to voice the praise of Creation, and so the Church does it on its behalf. This is why, in the book of Revelation, there is no temple in the heavenly city: there will no longer be a need for a separate community, the Church, to offer worship on behalf of the rest of humanity, because there, a renewed humanity itself will offer the worship it was always meant to. Worship, like the care of Creation, is primarily a human calling, not a Christian one. Christians just do it until the rest of humanity catches up.

We have drawn a picture of the Church as the community which Christ calls out from among the wider human race. He does it with a purpose: to bless the rest of humanity, so that in turn, it can play its divinely ordained role to fulfil the divine purpose for Creation. In the Church, we see the same pattern of mediating and perfecting that is the essence of Christ's priesthood, echoed and expressed in the Church's calling towards the rest of humanity.

Yet how does the Church play that role? How does the Church become the kind of community that is capable of blessing, interceding and offering worship for a human race that often fails to see its need for God? We have already seen how the earth, although created by God, still needs human mediation to enable it to grow into its full potential for beauty, joy and usefulness. In the same way, the human race needs the Church to remind it of its priestly calling, and to help it be ready to fulfil that calling. Likewise, the Church also needs help if it is to become what it has the potential to be. In each of these cases, a part of the whole is set apart to serve the whole. And this is exactly the role played by those whom the Church sets aside as its 'ministers', or to give them another name, its 'priests'.

6

The priesthood of ministers

——————•◆•——————

Just as the world needs humanity to enable it to be what it has the potential to be, and humanity needs the Church to fulfil its true purpose, so the Church needs its ministers, its 'priests', to become what it is intended to be in the divine plan.[1]

We discover the true role of ministers, clergy, priests, whatever we want to call them, when we relate them to this divine pattern of priesthood: the work of Christ who mediates God's love to the world, by which it is perfected in holiness and joy. Back in Chapter 3, we examined the case made by the sixteenth-century Reformers that priesthood should not be restricted to just a few officials within the Church, as it is Christ who is the true High Priest and the whole Church that is a priestly people. Their point was well made, especially in their context where 'priests' had often become exclusive channels to God, and the laity reduced to mere spectators of the activity of the clergy.

Maybe by now we can begin to see a different understanding of priesthood. God chooses a part to bless the whole. He chooses some to be the means by which the blessing he pours out in Christ reaches the rest. If that is true for the whole Creation (through humanity) and the whole of humanity (through the Church), then it is not surprising if he works in the same way towards the Church – blessing the Church through particular people called out from the whole to enable the Church to be what it is called to be, and do what it is called to do: to recall humanity to its priestly role in Creation. Calling clergy 'priests' does not take away from the priestly role of the whole Church, any more than calling the Church a 'kingdom of priests' takes away from Christ's priesthood. It is simply recognizing this pattern in the way God blesses the world. He does it through choosing a part to bless the whole. Priests in the Church are called to enable the Church to play its priestly role of declaring the praises of Jesus Christ, the true High Priest, so that in turn the rest of humanity might be restored to its proper priestly dignity, and the whole earth resound to the joy of God.

But as we start out on this part of the journey, the same questions need to be asked as before. If mediating, perfecting and offering are the heart of the priesthood of Christ – mediating God's presence and love to the world, bringing it to its full potential and offering it to God in worship – and we have seen that pattern at work in both the relationship between humanity and the wider Creation, and also between the Church and the human race, is the same pattern discernible between the Church and its priests?

Mediating

Clergy are human beings. That, hopefully, can be taken for granted (although some understandings of priesthood make them so distinct from humanity that they become almost like a separate race of people altogether, like the old Irish joke where there were three sets of public conveniences: one for Men, one for Women and a third for Priests).

Priests are also members of the Church, just like other Christians. This, however, is not something that can be taken for granted. Some older treatments of the theology of priesthood implied that priests somehow stood apart from the laity, as a kind of separate caste. For example, a classic work on the topic first published in 1897 by R. C. Moberly suggested that the Church acts through the priest, who exercises prerogatives that belong to the body as a whole.[2] For Moberly, it is a role that depends ultimately on the apostolate – the idea that the apostles passed on their authority to bishops and then presbyters/priests and deacons. Priests derive their authority, not from the Church as the priestly people of God, but from other ordained officials in the past. The primary identity of priests is therefore defined by their relationship to those who passed on the authority to them through the line of spiritual inheritance. As a result, they have a rather distant and remote relationship to Christ, the one who originally gave priestly authority, since their authority has been passed through numerous hands over the centuries, and only comes to them many times removed from the original source. There is little here of a sense of Christ's immediate, direct presence at the heart of the Church as its head, its overseer, its true High Priest. As Robin Greenwood puts it, this approach fosters a view of priestly ministers as 'individualistic, superordinate and separate from the laity'.[3]

More recent works on the topic emphasize the link between ministry and the Church, so that priesthood derives from the Church rather than the other way round.[4] The World Council of Churches' Lima document of 1982, *Baptism, Eucharist and Ministry*, which addressed areas of difference and growing agreement between various churches on questions of ecclesiology, laid the emphasis on the relationship between the ordained ministry and the Church, indicating their interdependence:

> The ordained ministry has no existence apart from the community. Ordained ministers can fulfil their calling only in and for the community. They cannot dispense with the recognition, the support and the encouragement of the community. The chief responsibility of the ordained ministry is to assemble and build up the body of Christ by proclaiming and teaching the Word of God, by celebrating the sacraments, and by guiding the life of the community in its worship, its mission and its caring ministry.[5]

Some Christians may be ordained priests but that does not mean they leave the ranks of the laity. They continue to be part of the *laos*, the 'people'; they are just set apart to be a distinct kind of lay person, with a distinct calling within the whole. They are simply called to a different order within the Church.

Baptism – the call to ministry

This takes us back to baptism as the true commissioning for ministry in the Church. When Jesus was baptized, he did not change ontologically – he was the Son of God before his baptism, just as he was afterwards. As we have seen already, his priesthood is eternal, not located in time. His baptism does not make him into the Son of God, or constitute him a priest. What it does is to reveal his true identity, which up to that point had remained hidden ('You are my Son, whom I love; with you I am well pleased' – Mark 1.11). It is also a commissioning for ministry. In all three synoptic Gospels in which it occurs, the baptism of Jesus is placed right at the start of his period of open preaching and healing, and marks the transition from his private life in Nazareth to his public ministry. As such, it also works as a commissioning and empowerment of him for that public ministry through the gift of the Holy Spirit.[6] The primary ceremony in which commissioning for ministry is given in the Christian Church is not ordination but baptism. That is fundamental. Every Christian has a ministry in and outside the Church, not just the clergy. To that extent, clergy are just like any other Christian, with a ministry to bear witness to Jesus Christ in whatever way they can. Ordination is a not a commissioning for ministry, but a setting apart for a particular kind of ministry, as we shall see.

Priests are therefore fully part of the Church, sharing in its life. Yet if mediation involves sharing in both sides of the parties between which they mediate, in what sense do priests share in the life of God?

In the past two chapters, we have sketched the relationships between God and the world (in which the priestly ministry of Christ is carried out through humanity), and between God and the human race (in which Christ's priestly ministry is carried out by the Church). In both cases, humanity and the Church share in the nature of the created side of this equation, but share by grace, or by calling, in the divine side of it. It is exactly the same in the relationships between the Church and its ministers. Ministers share by nature in the life of the Church. They are first and foremost baptized Christians. Yet at the same time, they share in the priestly ministry of Christ by grace, or by calling. Just as humans are called by God to be his means of blessing Creation, and the Church is called by God to be his means of blessing humanity, so priests are those called by God to be his means of blessing the Church.

Examples and images

1 Peter 5.1–4 is one of the main places in the New Testament where a distinctly presbyteral ministry is outlined:

> To the elders among you, I appeal as a fellow elder and a witness of Christ's sufferings who also will share in the glory to be revealed: be shepherds of God's flock that is under your care, watching over them – not because you must, but because you are willing, as God wants you to be; not pursuing dishonest gain, but eager to serve; not lording it over those entrusted to you, but being examples to the flock. And when the Chief Shepherd appears, you will receive the crown of glory that will never fade away.

There are two main emphases here worth noting carefully. One is the relationship of the elders with regards to Christ. They are to shepherd the flock (*poimanō*), exercising their ministry under the Chief Shepherd (*archipoimēn*). With a glance back to Calvin's idea of participating in the Sonship and therefore by extension also the priesthood of Christ, in the same way here, elders/ministers participate in the oversight that Christ has over his flock, the Church. The community that they care for is 'God's flock', not their own, and the ministry they exercise is Christ's ministry not their own. In other words, Christ the Chief Shepherd exercises his care and nurture of the flock through the elders/ministers, or 'priests' who are called to this shepherding, 'pastoral' ministry. Any ministry the elder offers that builds up the Church is not his or her own ministry, but is, in the fullest sense of the word, the ministry of Christ, building up the Church.

The other element is the call to be examples (*typoi*) to the flock. Elders/presbyters are, literally speaking, to be 'types' of Christ. Their calling is emphatically not to act like a Lord over the community (*katakurieuō* – the word carries the stem of *kurios* or 'Lord'), but instead they are to be images, pictures of Christ, just as Adam is a 'type' of Christ (Rom. 5.14). This language of 'example' or 'type' is common in the New Testament's picture of ministry and leadership (e.g. Phil 3.17; 2 Thess. 3.9; Titus 2.7). It conveys the idea of an image, or visible representation – the word *typos* could just as easily be used for a statue or image of a god in a pagan temple.[7] Elders are to be images of Christ, representatives of him and his ministry among the Church.

There is a tension to be guarded here. Priests are not the Lord. They are not the head of the Church. Nor are they the true High Priest. They are representatives of Christ, not identical with him. And it is vital to hold this dynamic. If the distinction between Christ and the priest is not maintained, that opens the door to the kind of abusive clerical domination that has been far too common in the history of the Church. Their ministry of oversight is to be exercised not primarily through authority or domination, but through example, lest they usurp the role of the Chief Shepherd. Yet if the close relation between the minister and Christ, that of representation, of example or image, is not maintained, then Christ's priestly ministry of preparing the Church to bless the rest of the human race cannot be fulfilled. Priests *represent* him in the truest sense of this word. Just as the Son was present in incarnate form in first-century Palestine, he is re-presented today within the Church, made present again, through the worship of the community, the celebration of the sacraments and the preaching of the Word, in all of which the priest plays a central role.

In other words, the priest is the one through whom Christ's oversight and care for the Church is expressed. Here again is that pattern of mediation, where God relates to the world through a part chosen out of the whole, in this case, through priests who are both a full part of the *laos*, the body of the Church itself, yet who at the same time represent Christ who works his priestly ministry through them.

Priests then stand in this particular place. They are fully part of the Church, no better nor worse than any other baptized Christian, not called to any exalted status, not called out of the laity, not elevated in any way – their roots are in the Church, just as the roots of humanity are in the earth and the Church is part of the human race. At the same time, they are called, summoned to be images, types, examples of Christ, representing him within the Church, just as humanity represents God within the world, and the Church represents God within humanity. They are called into this mediating role as agents of the priestly work of Christ.

Priesthood, the Church and the world

The focus then, for ordained priests or ministers, is not so much Creation, nor the rest of society, but the Church. John Chrysostom writes of the priest: 'One thing alone he must consider: the edification of the Church.'[8] Miroslav Volf develops an understanding of ordained ministry based on the common baptism of all Christians, but with particular charismata bestowed on some for this particular ministry, similar to the idea we have been sketching. He suggests that 'the specific element attaching to the charismata of office is their reference to the entirety of the local church'.[9] It is a reminder that the focus of ordained ministry is first and foremost the Church: it is to enable the Church to be the Church.

The focus of ordained ministry is therefore only indirectly towards the world. In the divine economy we have been exploring here, it is the Church that serves the rest of humanity. Priests primarily serve the Church, so that the Church can truly be itself. However, this is not because the world does not matter. It is precisely *because* the world matters. The Church as a whole, not just priests themselves, is called to be a missionary, evangelistic people, reminding the rest of the human race of its true calling: to protect and nurture Creation towards its final end and true joy. Priests are those Christians called out from among the Church, to enable the Church to be what it is called to be: a priestly community that is capable of reminding humanity of its true calling and identity.

So why do we ordain people to some ministries but not others? Why are 'deacons', 'priests' and 'ministers' ordained, and yet those called to a ministry of encouragement or administration or evangelism are not? The answer is that priests are those called specifically to enable the ministry of the encouragers, the administrators and the evangelists. Their focus is on the operation of the whole Church – enabling the whole Church in all its parts, with all its gifts, to fulfil its divine calling.

If this is true, then the growth of the Church matters. Sometimes, the language of church growth is criticized because the focus of the Church is not its own growth, but its calling to the world. In a similar vein, clergy often feel that the growth of the Church is somehow an unworthy goal, in that numbers in church, bums on pews, is less important than community involvement. Yet if the primary focus of ordained ministry is first the Church, so that the Church can be a blessing to the world, then the actual growth of the Church matters, for two reasons.

First, growth matters because the Church's calling is to bring restoration and healing to damaged and broken people, so that they become capable again of giving themselves for the care and nurture of Creation. Every time a person encounters the love of Christ through the Church, and in that love finds healing, forgiveness and new purpose, the Church is fulfilling its true vocation. At the same time, the building up of the Church into a viable, strong community, confident in its own faith and identity, renders it better able to fulfil that calling corporately, rather than just individually. The growth of the Church matters because humanity and the rest of Creation matter, and the health of the Church is a vital part of the divine conspiracy of blessing.

Perfecting

Priesthood is about perfecting, bringing the divine blessing to bear, so that things are brought to maturity. The calling of priests is to work for the perfecting, the maturing of the Church into a body fit for purpose.

How then do Christian priests fulfil this role towards the Church? The main word used in the New Testament for oversight, or leadership within the Church is *presbuteros*, commonly translated 'elder'. Elders are those who 'direct the affairs of the church' (1 Tim. 5.17). 'Elders' and 'overseers' (*episkopoi*) often seem to be interchangeable terms, but the focus of both is the welfare of the Church:

> Appoint elders in every town, as I directed you. An elder must be blameless, faithful to his wife, a man whose children believe and are not open to the charge of being wild and disobedient. Since an overseer manages God's household, he must be blameless.
>
> (Titus 1.5–7)

Just as the calling of the human race is to protect and nurture Creation (Gen. 2.15), the calling of the minister is to protect and nurture the Church. This dual emphasis, on nurture and protection, is exactly what we find when we dig a little deeper into the New Testament writings on the leadership of the Christian community. And it is carried out through a number of key elements: elders or priests nurture and protect the Church through their example, teaching, care and leadership.

Example

We have already seen how the predominant note struck when the New Testament discusses presbyteral ministry is that of example. Ministers are to be reminders of Christ the true High Priest by simply reminding people of him in the pattern of their behaviour. This note of example draws attention to the fact that priestly ministry in the Church is much more than a job or a function. It flows out of the very being of ministers, and their relationship to the Christ who works through them. In particular, it flows out of the life of the priest in prayer.

As we have seen, clergy are first and foremost baptized Christians before they are ordained ministers. But as ordained, set apart, called out from the main body of the Church for the sake of the whole, they are called to be exemplary Christians. That, of course, does not mean being perfect Christians, but exemplary, in the sense that if others were to watch and follow their actions and way of life, they would not go far wrong. In the last chapter, we suggested that Christ exercises his priestly ministry through the Church's intercession, blessing, sacrifice and evangelism. The individual priest is to be an example to the Church, a 'type' or image of Christ by displaying these very things in his or her own life.

The priest is to be someone who prays, interceding for the Church, its members and the world, joining in the prayer of the Son to the Father in what Barth calls our 'modest participation in the work of Jesus Christ'.[10] Priests are also to bless, and to be a blessing, through acts of kindness and generosity. They are also to live a sacrificial life, one which is marked by the proper disciplining of desire, the practice of spiritual exercises that serve to direct the heart towards what will alone bring it happiness and satisfaction: God himself. They are also to be individuals who cultivate friendships and relationships beyond the bounds of the Church. This is not just for the sake of evangelizing the people they know (although any Christian will want to share the good news of Christ with friends), but so that they are able to know the world outside the Church well enough to be able to encourage the rest of the Church to bear witness creatively and intelligently to Jesus Christ.[11]

Before thinking about any particular tasks of ministry, comes the question of the life of the minister. Of course, the ministry of the word and sacraments does not ultimately depend on the life of the priest: as St Augustine argued in his debates with the Donatists, just as the sun can shine through a dirty sewer, the grace of Christ can flow through an unworthy and sinful priest. Having said that, priests who are vain, conceited or gossips are unlikely to gain much hearing for their public teaching or wider ministry, and for good reason. If the point of Christian ministry is that Christ can exercise his priestly work within the Church, priests who draw attention away from Christ and on to themselves will prevent the growth of the Church into maturity, rather than promoting it. The Church needs visible reminders of Christ, its true High Priest, the one through whom it has access to the Father.

Example works both as protection and nurture. It protects in that it provides a kind of rule of life, a picture of Christ-like life that keeps the Church from straying too far from him. It is why clergy sometimes can be expected to strive for a higher or more demanding moral path than lay people, not because they are more important, but because the rest of the Church tends to follow where its leaders go. At the same time, example serves to nurture the Church, beckoning it to Christ-like life, showing it a worked example of what a full human life looks like, one that reflects the nature and character of Jesus Christ.

Word, sacrament and Spirit

Jürgen Moltmann, following Calvin, reminds us that 'the church is where Christ is'.[12] The Church is found wherever the Risen Christ is present and people gather around him. Yet how do we know Christ is present? Where does Christ's presence 'show up' within the world? John Calvin's well-known identification of the marks of the Church gives a working definition: 'Wherever we see the Word of God purely preached and heard, and the sacraments administered according to Christ's institution, there, it is not to be doubted, a church of God exists.'[13]

Christ is present in his word and sacraments, and when people who encounter them are enabled by the Holy Spirit to respond to them in faith.[14] Now if that is how Christ makes himself present

123

to us, then we begin to see how important the ministry of the word and sacraments is, along with the ministry of the Holy Spirit through them. Priests have a particular calling to teach the faith and entrust it to others:

> If you point these things out to the brothers and sisters, you will be a good minister of Christ Jesus, nourished on the truths of the faith and of the good teaching that you have followed ... Command and teach these things ... Until I come, devote yourself to the public reading of Scripture, to preaching and to teaching.
>
> (1 Tim 4.6, 11–13; see also 2 Tim. 2.2; 4.2)

Even overseers (*episkopoi*) have the teaching ministry as one of their main functions (Titus 1.9; 2.1). The ministry of the word is the ministry of constantly reminding the Church of its true identity and calling. This method of leadership, of course, is not unique to the Church. Charles Handy, one of the most influential writers on management and leadership in recent years (who is also the son of a clergyman, so he knows a bit about leadership in the Church!) writes: 'The leader's first job is to be a missionary, to remind people what is special about them and their institutions.'[15]

The priest bears the responsibility of recalling the Church constantly to its priestly calling. Priests remind the Church of its rootedness in the rest of humanity, ensuring it doesn't become remote, patronizing or condescending in its attitude towards the community around it. At the same time, priests have to remind the Church of its divine calling, to be the agent through which Christ does his work of restoring humanity to its place within the created order. Most of all, priests are to remind the Church of Christ, its true High Priest, its true Head. They do this through constant, intelligent reading of Scripture, the Church's book, the text that the Church recognizes as its title deeds. Priesthood demands of ministers that they be good theologians, regular readers of Scripture and the great tradition of Christian theology. They need, in other words, to know the deep structure of Christian faith and its view of the world. They need to understand the pattern of divine interaction with the world, who God is, what the world is and the place of humanity and the Church within it.

Teaching has a protective function. There will be internal threats, when church members lie to each other or fall out over trifles, when those in some kind of authority try to use power inappropriately and when abusive behaviour is discovered. Similarly, there will be times when the Church forgets itself and its story. The Church has at various points been in danger of misreading its true calling, or the nature and shape of the gospel it is called to proclaim in both its words and its deeds. At those points, the person charged with responsibility over the Church needs the courage and the strength to step in and protect it from internal dangers. This is why priests need to be theologically trained and alert, to know the deep structure and fabric of the gospel so they can recognize when one of its threads starts to be pulled in a way that could lead to the unravelling of the whole.

At other times, the threats will be from without. The Church will always have its opponents, some obvious and direct, some less obvious and subtle. Sometimes it will be political manoeuvres that seek to limit the Church's freedom to live and proclaim its gospel. Sometimes it will be intellectual attacks by whichever group opposes the Christian Church at any one time. At other times, and in some parts of the world more than others, it will be the threat of physical attack or violence. The priest is called to protect the Church from harm, ensuring he or she does that in a way that is in harmony with the very gospel being defended – not using violence against violence, but 'tak[ing] captive every thought to make it obedient to Christ', or suffering where need be (2 Cor. 10.5).

Through this ministry of the Word, Christ becomes present. The other way in which Christ 'shows up' in the Church is in the sacraments of baptism and the Eucharist. In water, and in bread and wine which are set apart and prayed over that it might be a sign for us of Christ and his grace, Christ makes himself available to us. Quite how this happens is, of course, subject to debate in the Church, and there is no time to go into that argument here. However, whether understood as some kind of substantial presence, or in a more memorial way, pointing to Christ and his sacrifice on the cross or to the eschatological banquet to which we are invited, Holy Communion is just that: a holy communion of the community with one another and with Christ who lives within his Church.

Calvin's definition of the Church (see page 123) requires not just Word and sacrament: it also requires the activity of the Spirit in enabling people to see and hear the word and presence of Christ in the community as they gather around the Word and share bread and wine. The minister has the responsibility also of encouraging expectation of the Spirit's work in and through the Word and sacraments, but also beyond them, in the prayers of members of the Church for one another, where we minister Christ to one another, making space for the Spirit who blows where he wills.[16]

All this requires a willingness to be repetitive. Reminding the community of its calling to be a 'light to the nations', to bless the rest of humanity so that it can in turn be a blessing to the world needs doing again and again; as does the repeated ritual of the sacraments; as does the ministry of the Spirit, however conceived. Yet this is precisely what is needed if the Church is to be itself, to be what it is called to be by Christ.[17] This ministry of Word, sacrament and Spirit protects the Church by keeping it faithful to its true identity, preventing it from losing its soul. St Paul's speech to the Ephesian presbyters emphasizes this same note of protection:

> Keep watch over yourselves and all the flock of which the Holy Spirit has made you overseers. Be shepherds of the church of God, which he bought with his own blood. I know that after I leave, savage wolves will come in among you and will not spare the flock. Even from your own number men will arise and distort the truth in order to draw away disciples after them. So be on your guard!
>
> (Acts 20.28–31)

On the other hand, this ministry of Word, sacrament and Spirit also nurtures the Church by providing the spiritual food by which it grows into full maturity, full perfection in Christ. These are the means by which Christ does his work of mediating, perfecting and offering in the Church, and it is the task of the priest to ensure these are fully in place, given free rein to do their work.

Care

The Church is ultimately cared for by Christ (Eph. 5.29). It lives under his protection. And yet, in what is by now a familiar pattern, this care is expressed through the ministers called to re-present him and his love to the Church. The pastoral image of shepherd is often used in the context of the role of the presbyter. The first letter of Peter 5, a classic text referring to the presbyters, says: 'Be shepherds of God's flock that is under your care, watching over them – not because you must, but because you are willing, as God wants you to be . . . being examples to the flock' (1 Pet. 5.2–3).

In the letter of James, the elders are specifically enjoined to pray for and lay hands on the sick (5.14). In other words, one of the primary functions of the priest is to ensure the Christian community is a place of care and love. That does not necessarily mean the clergy providing all the pastoral care themselves. It does mean ensuring that the Church is a place in which the love and care of God can be found and experienced.

If the Church's particular vocation is as we have described it here, then the ministry of simple and practical love and care is as vital to the Church's identity as the ministry of Word, sacrament and Spirit. Christ is the true High Priest who mediates God's love to the world. The love of God is, strictly speaking, the love of the Father for the Son, and of the Son for the Father, into which the Holy Spirit invites us and the whole Creation.[18] What people need is not the love and care of the Church, but the love and care of God. However, the Church extends its care in the name of Christ himself, so that the love it offers becomes a sign and expression of the love of God.

The minister bears the responsibility of making sure that the church is a place where the weak and vulnerable find care and protection, not damage and abuse. The church can only be a reminder, or representative, of Christ by being a community marked by love, gentleness and respect, the kind that God himself shows us in Christ.

Leadership

The last function of the 'elder' in the texts of the New Testament is that of leadership. First Timothy 5.17 says: 'The elders who direct the affairs of the church well are worthy of double honour.' The Greek word used here is *prohistēmi*, which means to manage, govern, direct or rule. Another verb used in this connection is *ēgeomai*, referring to 'leaders, who spoke the word of God to you' (Heb. 13.7). The next chapter will look more closely at the concept of priestly leadership, in the light of the framework explored in this book, but as this chapter closes, here are a few observations on this theme.

One of the most influential books on mission written in the twentieth century was by a little-known missionary to Northern China, Roland Allen. He lived from 1868 to 1947, and the book was published in 1912.[19] At the time, it didn't gain a great deal of attention, but it has been described since as something of a time bomb in thinking on mission, leadership and ecclesiology. Allen looked at the methods of missionary agencies in the nineteenth century and beyond, and noticed a pattern. The first stage was that a mission agency would raise money at home to send a missionary, who would then build a school or hospital and church. At this stage, the missionary would basically do everything: keep the purse strings, administer the funds, decide on who should be baptized, adjudicate on any issues that came up in the life of the burgeoning community. The second stage was to bring the 'natives' alongside to teach them how to do all that the missionary had initially done. The final stage was the intention to retire into the background, ideally leaving behind a fully indigenous church.

However, as he surveyed the record of this strategy, it seemed distinctly unsuccessful. Sixty years or more later, mission stations were still running with huge investment from the home country, with continued appeals for funds, and the locals reluctant to take responsibility. When missionaries went home on furlough, very often things collapsed, and when they returned, either nothing much had happened, or the structures that had been set up had fallen apart. The churches left behind by this method also had little missionary impulse themselves.

Allen then examined the missionary methods of St Paul. They were strikingly different. Paul only spent between six and eighteen months in any one place, and moved on fairly quickly, but he still managed to leave behind fully functioning, self-supporting churches. Allen observed how Paul's approach was to leave behind a number of key features, including some basic teaching, consisting of a rudimentary creed, the orally delivered stories of Jesus, and especially the account of his death and resurrection. He taught them to baptize and celebrate the Lord's Supper. He appointed elders, whose qualifications were largely moral and spiritual not intellectual, and of course he left behind the Old Testament Scriptures and a growing body of material which in time grew into the New Testament: letters and snippets of stories of Jesus.

Paul gave them no set liturgical forms, no elaborate church order, structures or architecture. He refused to administer their funds. He allowed the churches to decide who to baptize. Discipline was not laid down in advance, but dealt with as issues arose. He refused to subject local churches to the authority of the 'mother church', whether in Jerusalem or anywhere else for that matter. Paul's approach was minimalist, and yet he achieved in a few months what nineteenth-century missions had failed to do over fifty or sixty years: produce independent churches with vibrant life and missionary vision.

Allen reckoned that Paul's secret was this very minimalism. He refused to get in the way. He encouraged Christians to take responsibility for their own church right from the start. As a result, they 'owned' the church, and consequently it grew. Modern missions had done the opposite, fostering a sense of dependency on the ordained leader appointed from afar. Allen thought there were two main reasons why the modern missionary movement did this, and both amounted to a lack of trust.

One was a lack of trust in local Christians. The paternalistic Western imperialism that often sadly accompanied such missionary activity thought that the natives were just not up to it. More profoundly, however, it was due to a lack of trust in the Holy Spirit. To exercise this kind of leadership required a deep trust in the Holy Spirit's work in the life of the Church, the Spirit's ability to guide and sustain it. Paul, Allen argued, had this trust in the Spirit of Christ to guide the Church himself, rather than trying to do it for him. Without such trust, the life of the Church is stifled.

The inevitable question arose: what if they get it wrong? And the answer is, of course, that they did! Paul's letters to the Galatian and Corinthian churches are painful testimony to the fact that they often did get it wrong. However, on Allen's reading, Paul was much happier letting them make mistakes than stifling life, quenching the Spirit. Of course, Paul did not leave them to their own devices. He prayed, visited, wrote constantly; but essentially, he left it to them.

Allen overstates his case at points, but it is a salutary approach. This is a leadership that defers to Christ's leadership of the Church through the Spirit. If the priestly ministry is really Christ's ministry at work through them, then a key element of the ministry of priests will simply be to stop getting in the way. Allen wrote at one point:

> I never ask anyone to do anything and consequently I do not get a yes or a no. I say what seems to me obviously true, but they do not know what to do about it. One day someone will see what

action is demanded, and perhaps screw up their courage to take it. If I were out to organize & lead, that would be different, but as you well know I long ago determined that was not to be the way of the Spirit for me. If any man answers, 'That is out of date' or 'Times have changed', I can only repeat, 'This is the way of Christ and His Apostles', and leave him to face that issue.[20]

Allen's approach, of a leadership that sees its primary role as telling the truth, reminding the community of what it is meant to be, and allowing Christ to do his work in the Church by the Spirit, points the way to a genuinely Christian approach to leadership, one we will explore in more detail in the next chapter.

Offering

In the context of writing about the relationships between husband and wife, St Paul writes:

> Christ loved the church and gave himself up for her to make her holy, cleansing her by the washing with water through the word, and to present her to himself as a radiant church, without stain or wrinkle or any other blemish, but holy and blameless.
>
> (Eph. 5.25–27)

This is, of course, Christ doing his priestly work presenting the Church as an offering to God. And yet Paul can also describe his own ministry in the same terms. Echoing the same marital language he writes: 'I promised you to one husband, to Christ, so that I might present you as a pure virgin to him' (2 Cor. 11.2). As he writes to the Galatians, he strikes the note of a deep concern for the growth and formation of the Church into Christ-like life: 'My dear children, for whom I am again in the pains of childbirth until Christ is formed in you' (Gal. 4.19).

In 2 Corinthians 4, a passage where Paul reflects on his own ministry with regard to the church in Corinth, ministry is conceived again as a sacrifice by the minister for the life and welfare of the Church:

> Death is at work in us, but life is at work in you . . . All this is for
> your benefit, so that the grace that is reaching more and more
> people may cause thanksgiving to overflow to the glory of God.
>
> (2 Cor. 4.12–15)

This passage actually widens the scope to the entire schema laid
out in this book: the minister serves the Church, so that the Church
causes people to give thanks, which then redounds to the glory
of God.

Paul seemed to see his whole ministry, its sufferings, its sacrifice,
its hard work, as directed towards the same goal: the perfecting
of the Church so that it can be an offering of worship to God.

> I fill up in my flesh what is still lacking in regard to Christ's afflic-
> tions, for the sake of his body, which is the church. I have become
> its servant by the commission God gave me to present to you the
> word of God in its fulness – the mystery that has been kept hidden
> for ages and generations, but is now disclosed to the Lord's people.
> To them God has chosen to make known among the Gentiles the
> glorious riches of this mystery, which is Christ in you, the hope
> of glory. He is the one we proclaim, admonishing and teaching
> everyone with all wisdom, so that we may present everyone fully
> mature in Christ. To this end I strenuously contend with all the
> energy Christ so powerfully works in me.   (Col. 1.24–29)

Here are the notes we have been striking, all in harmonious
symphony. Christian ministry is 'for the sake of the church'.
Paul proclaims Christ the unique Son, the High Priest, drawing
attention not to himself or any other clerical figure for that matter.
And the goal is to 'present everyone fully mature in Christ'. The
word translated 'fully mature' is, of course, *teleios*, the word often
translated 'perfect'. The goal of Christian ministry is nothing less
than the perfecting of the Church.

Christian ministry is seen as carrying out Christ's priestly work
of offering the Church back to God as a perfect offering. Paul
does what Christ does. Or to put it better, Christ does his work
of perfecting the Church through his servant Paul.

Christian priests are expected to nurture a deep love for the Church, because only with such a love can they work for its good. Priests who dislike or distrust or despise the Church can never serve it. They will certainly never change it. This calling is precisely to love the Church and give oneself for it, so that it can be presented to God, fully fit for purpose, drawing the human race back to where it was always meant to be, in fellowship with God, enabling the whole Creation to resound to the praise and joy of God.

7

Priestly leadership

---·◆·◆·◆---

Surveys of the experience of parish clergy or local ministers suggest the pressures on them are significant. The job is relatively poorly paid, so that while the stress levels can be comparable to other professions, there is little possibility of compensating with expensive holidays, nannies for the children or help around the house. It is a job that is never finished. How do you know when you have achieved something? Unlike an architect who finishes a project, a salesperson who clinches a deal, or a bus driver who successfully guides a vehicle to the end of the journey, it is hard to know when the job has been completed. There might be a feeling of completion after a sermon has been preached or a service led, but much of the ongoing pastoral and managerial work of clergy is never quite over and often relatively unfocused. Clergy are expected to be educators, pastors, inspirational figures, community leaders, conductors of rites of passage, fundraisers, chairs of meetings, counsellors, theologians and at the same time managers of what is effectively a small business, with budgets, targets and often very few additional paid staff. At the same time, their role within society has changed dramatically.

In particular, clergy are now often expected to be leaders as well as priests. Conferences, books, online talks and blogs on Christian leadership abound, all of which often add to the sense of expectation. Yet it is a development that has not gone unchallenged.[1] Talk of leadership is not uncontested, and often the protest is raised in the name of a priestly model of ministry: that clergy are primarily called to be priests, not leaders. Now some of these older models have themselves been critiqued, often from the same sources,[2] but how do we put together talk of leadership with the approach to priesthood we have been exploring here?

As we saw at the end of the last chapter, the concept of someone who 'directs the affairs of the church' is not foreign to the New Testament. Priests do exercise some form of leadership within the church: they are called to 'direct its affairs'. The question is how are they to do that in the light of the role we have been exploring for them in the last chapter and throughout this book? What kind of leaders are they to be? To shun the language of leadership altogether seems unnecessarily pedantic; however, one way of describing the difference between Christian models of leadership in the Church and more secular patterns is to describe a specifically priestly form of leadership – one that is deeply conscious that it serves and exists only in the light of the priesthood of Christ, the only true Leader.

Leadership in the Bible

In early Christian texts, we find a bewildering range of titles for various 'leaders' within the Christian community. Hippolytus' 'Apostolic Tradition' – usually dated around AD 235 and reflecting the organization of the church in Rome around that time – lists bishops, deacons, presbyters, confessors, readers and sub-deacons. Other texts speak of prophets, doorkeepers, acolytes, exorcists and many more. One word is never used, however, either in the New Testament or, to my knowledge, in early Christian literature, and that is the normal word for 'leaders' in the Graeco-Roman empire: *Archōn*.

The word is used in the New Testament, to be sure, but never for Christian leaders. First, it is used to describe the authority figures in the Roman empire, for example in Romans 13.3 ('rulers hold no terror for those who do right, but for those who do wrong') or in Acts 16.19 ('they seized Paul and Silas and dragged them into the market-place to face the authorities'). Paul in 1 Corinthians 2.6 uses the same word for the political leaders in the empire: 'We do, however, speak a message of wisdom among the mature, but not the wisdom of this age or of the rulers of this age,[3] who are coming to nothing.' Second, it is used for Jewish leaders. The high priest in Jerusalem is described as an *Archōn* (Acts 23.5), and Josephus, the first-century Jewish historian uses the word in exactly the same way to describe Jewish religious officials. Third, it is used to describe demonic powers. Satan, or Beelzebub, is regularly described as the 'Prince of demons', with this same word being used.[4]

When it comes to Christian usage of this common word for leader/authority/governor, there is a deafening silence. This, it seems, was a word the early Christians avoided like the plague. Now this makes us realize than when we speak of leadership we have to be cautious, as the Scriptures display a marked reticence about such language, a reticence that had deep roots.

Biblical ambivalence

The Hebrew Scriptures contain a deep ambivalence about leadership and authority. In 1 Samuel 8, the people of Israel ask for a king, so they can be just like the other nations, with a dynamic hero to lead them into battle. Samuel the prophet speaks to God, who reluctantly grants them one, but with the proviso to Samuel that 'it is not you they have rejected, but they have rejected me as their king' (v. 7). For Israel to adopt a king actually means a rejection of God, because he is their true king. Samuel then warns the people what a king will do:

> This is what the king who will reign over you will claim as his rights: he will take your sons and make them serve with his chariots and horses, and they will run in front of his chariots. Some he will assign to be commanders of thousands and commanders of fifties, and others to plough his ground and reap his harvest, and still others to make weapons of war and equipment for his chariots. He will take your daughters to be perfumers and cooks and bakers. He will take the best of your fields and vineyards and olive groves and give them to his attendants. He will take a tenth of your grain and of your vintage and give it to his officials and

attendants. Your male and female servants and the best of your cattle and donkeys he will take for his own use. He will take a tenth of your flocks, and you yourselves will become his slaves. When that day comes, you will cry out for relief from the king you have chosen, but the LORD will not answer you in that day.

(1 Sam. 8.11–18)

Ever since this episode, we find a deep uncertainty about the idea of kingship. Alongside Samuel's suspicion there is Hosea's hostility. Later, in the eighth century BC, on the eve of exile, looking back on a period when Israel's kings did exactly what Samuel had prophesied, the prophet Hosea says: 'they set up kings without my consent; they choose princes without my approval' (Hos. 8.4).

At the same time, however, we see in the Psalms a vision of kingship redeemed. The psalmists often praise the kings of Israel. Kings are granted the protection of God:

> Through the victories you gave, his glory is great;
> you have bestowed on him splendour and majesty.
> Surely you have granted him unending blessings
> and made him glad with the joy of your presence.
> For the king trusts in the LORD;
> through the unfailing love of the Most High
> he will not be shaken. (Ps. 21.5–7)

The king is also praised as the bringer of justice. Psalm 72 is an extended prayer for the king, desiring his long life and prosperity, on the basis that he is the one who will deliver the poor, rather than oppressing or exploiting them, as some of the ancient kings had done.

> For he will deliver the needy who cry out,
> the afflicted who have no one to help.
> He will take pity on the weak and the needy
> and save the needy from death.
> He will rescue them from oppression and violence,
> for precious is their blood in his sight.
>
> (Ps. 72.12–14)

In other words, in the Old Testament we see a vision of the deep dangers of leadership, and its potential for abuse and injustice. Yet we also see a vision of what it could be, reshaped and redeemed. And underlying this ambivalence is one core principle: that God is the true king.[5]

This is a fact that relativizes all other kingship. Because God is king, all earthly authority is derived not absolute. An examination of other rulers in the ancient world – whether ancient Near Eastern potentates in Egypt, Babylon or further afield, Chinese emperors or later rulers of the Hellenistic or Roman empires – reveals a common theme of the absolute authority of the human ruler, who was often seen as an embodiment of the gods. This was an ideology that validated their every move, and gave them absolute control over their subjects, having literally the power of life or death over them.

The Old Testament laid the foundations for a political theology that undermined all that. Kings could be, and regularly were, challenged by prophets who called them to account in the name of the God that gave them any authority they held. In the New Testament, this same theme is radicalized into at times a kind of civil disobedience ('we must obey God rather than human beings' – Acts 5.29). Romans 13 is a passage where St Paul famously encourages obedience to authority, a note that has caused much heart-searching in later Christian times. However, at the beginning of what seems a fairly conservative line on obeying political authorities stands a truly revolutionary statement: 'there is no authority except that which God has established' (v. 1). In other words, no human authority is absolute. All is penultimate not ultimate. Every human ruler, however powerful, however exalted, is accountable, and will be called to account before the Creator.

In the modern Western world, of course, we no longer have kings, we have democracies. The Social Contract, the idea developed by such political thinkers as Thomas Hobbes, Jean-Jacques Rousseau and John Locke which helped pave the way for modern democracy, posits a contract between the ruler and the people.

This is nothing else but a version of the basic Judaeo-Christian idea that power and authority are derived, not absolute. In this version, authority is still derived, but now, not so much from God, but from the people. The idea could not have developed without this background in the Bible, the notion that all human authority comes from God and it is only ever delegated, not given to human beings.

Contemporary models

It was not just their reading of the Bible that led the early Christians to be wary of the contemporary language of leadership. The available models of leadership were not exactly encouraging either. In the first few centuries of the Church's existence, there was no doubt where ultimate power lay: in Rome. The power of the emperors was total. Such power usually came from inherited wealth, noble ancestry or military prowess and glory. The basic agreed understanding was that emperors could do what they wanted – they could enact whatever laws they chose, sleep with whoever they wanted, execute whoever crossed their path; until, that is, they were unseated by a coup or rebellion, at which point someone else adopted the same approach. The basis of imperial power was usually control over the armies of the empire, and therefore leadership was always connected in some way with violence, and always brought huge financial riches and personal wealth. As a result, this form of leadership within the empire quickly turned into a means of abuse, or domination. No wonder the author of 1 Peter felt he needed to remind the leaders of his churches that they were not to be 'pursuing dishonest gain . . . not lording it over those entrusted to you' (1 Pet. 5.2–3). It sounds like a deliberate reference to the way imperial power was used!

It may well be that one of the reasons *Archōn* was not used by early Church writers was because this is how *Archontes* usually behaved, and they wanted none of it. It is a little like what happened to German usage of the word *Führer*. Before the Nazi period, it was a word used commonly for 'leader' or 'guide'. Since it became the word most associated with Adolf Hitler, Germans have been much less likely to use it, especially in political contexts, preferring words such as *Leiter* instead. Words can go bad on you. They can fade from use because of unfortunate connotations. And this is what seems to have happened in early Christian circles with the word *Archōn*. It conjured up an abusive and damaging picture of leadership that they wanted to avoid as much as they possibly could.

Jesus the Head

With these two factors in the background, we can move on to the main reason why the early Christians were reluctant to call each other leaders: their conviction that the position was already taken. Just as the Samuel tradition in the Old Testament had insisted that God was the true king and therefore there could not be a king in Israel, so the New Testament writers were convinced that Jesus was the true leader of the Church – he was the one to whom authority had been given, and therefore they could never talk of others in the same breath.

Wolfhart Pannenberg is perhaps the twentieth-century theologian who most clearly pointed to the one fact from which all Christology must emerge: the resurrection. If God raised Jesus Christ from the dead, then he is the Lord of heaven and earth. The resurrection casts its light back over the pre-Easter life of Jesus and vindicates it once and for all. As Pannenberg put it: 'Jesus' unity with God [is] established in his resurrection from the dead with the resulting divine approval of his pre-Easter activity.'[6] All that Jesus was and did before Easter is suddenly seen in a new light after the resurrection. This Jesus, who healed the sick, taught the simple, raised the dead and who himself died on a cross, is the Lord of heaven and earth.

The 'Great Commission' at the climax of Matthew's Gospel strikes this note, that as the Risen One, who is now to ascend to the right hand of the Father, he is truly the Lord, with the claim that 'All authority in heaven and on earth has been given to me' (Matt. 28.18). We have seen already how the ascension completes the picture of Christ's unique high priesthood – the ascension is the coronation of Jesus Christ as the true Prophet, Priest and King.

This was the heart of the early Christians' gospel. For St Paul, to be saved, you need to 'declare with your mouth "Jesus is Lord," and believe in your heart that God raised him from the dead' (Rom. 10.9). However, this was not just seen as a kind of spiritual lordship in another separate or parallel sphere from the political and earthy realities of life in first-century Greek or Roman cities. This claim had a political and temporal dimension, which led the early Christians to claim that if Jesus Christ is Lord, then Caiaphas, Pilate, Caesar, or any other human ruler for that matter, is not. As the Jews of Thessalonica said about the Christians in their midst: 'They are all defying Caesar's decrees, saying that there is another king, one called Jesus' (Acts 17.7). Or as Peter and the other disciples saw quite clearly, when it came to a clash, as it would from time to time, there was no question where their loyalties were to lie: 'We must obey God rather than human beings' (Acts 5.29).

When it came to the Church, this was fleshed out in the idea that Christ is the only true Head of the Church. The Epistle to the Ephesians states it in uncompromising terms: 'Christ is the head of the church, his body, of which he is the Saviour' (Eph. 5.23). Colossians is, if anything, even stronger: 'he is the head of the body, the church; he is the beginning and the firstborn from among the dead, so that in everything he might have the supremacy' (Col 1.18).

This is, at the end of the day, the reason why the early Christians shunned the language of leadership in the Church: because there is only one true Leader, and that is Jesus Christ. And just as in the Old Testament there lurked the strong fear that the setting up of kings would lead to people setting themselves up as rivals to God, the same fear was felt in the New Testament Church as well. After all, it was Jesus himself who contrasted what his disciples' approach to leadership should be with that of the Jewish leaders of his time: 'But you are not to be called "Rabbi", for you have one Teacher, and you are all brothers. And do not call anyone on earth "father", for you have one Father, and he is in heaven' (Matt. 23.8–9).

Our journey so far has emphasized the central New Testament insight that Jesus is the true High Priest, the one who holds God and his Creation together, the one who has assumed human nature, perfected it and taken it back to the right hand of the Father. We can only ever do these things in him, not apart from him. So if that is that case, why do we still speak of leadership if Jesus is the true Leader?

Leadership in the shadow (or light) of Jesus

Sometimes in Christian leadership manuals, we find the advice that we need to model our leadership on that of Christ. In a way that is partly true, but it carries the possibility of a dangerous misunderstanding at the same time. If it is taken to mean that Jesus is a kind of example of a good leader, someone we might choose to imitate, just as we might imitate Winston Churchill, John F. Kennedy, Nelson Mandela or any of the other great leaders of our times, then we have made a big mistake. Just as we have seen that we do not have any separate priesthood from Christ but only participate by grace in his priestly activity, in the same way, priests or ministers do not lead in parallel to Christ, using him as a useful and illuminating example for leadership, gaining a few helpful tips from him along the way. Jesus is not a leadership guru. Instead, whatever leadership anyone exercises in the Church is derived from Christ, and serves and bears witness to his headship, or leadership, of the Church. The great danger for Christian leaders is that they usurp Christ, just as effectively as Israelite kings or Roman emperors did.

So why then do we speak of leadership at all, given that the Bible and the early Christians were so wary of it? For the same reason as we talk of priests, even though the New Testament and Christian history also insists that Jesus is the only true Priest: because we are invited to share in his leadership just as we are invited to share in his priesthood. He chooses to exercise his leadership over the Church through people chosen for that task, just as he exercises his priestly work within the world through humanity and through the Church. As we saw in the last chapter, there are those who are called to be 'elders', to 'direct the affairs of the church', those who are called to be shepherds of the flock of God 'that is under [their] care', never as a replacement for the leadership of Christ, but always as serving that very leadership. They are called to be the instruments through which his headship of the Church is exercised. Christ exercises his leadership precisely through the leadership of his ministers, who represent and mediate his rule to the Church and who perfect it so it can be offered back to God, fit for the purpose for which it was originally called. This means, however, a very different kind of leadership is required in the Christian Church, compared to other contexts.

Priestly leadership is a means of divine blessing

The pattern of priesthood we have been exploring in this book is about the way in which God blesses the world. He chooses humanity to be his means of blessing Creation. He chooses the Church to be the means of blessing humanity. He chooses priests to be the means of blessing the Church. In each case, the divine blessing is channelled through a part to the whole, not for the privilege of the part, but for the good of the whole. Priesthood is about blessing, working for the good, the perfection of the whole, so it can be offered back to God in intimate union and fellowship.

This means that priestly leadership can be seen primarily as a means of divine blessing for the Church. If a person is called to leadership within the Church they are called not to privileged status or grandeur, but to be one of the primary ways in which God means to bless his Church. That perspective can transform both the leaders themselves (nipping in the bud any lurking temptation to lordly behaviour or domineering condescension) and the Church (viewing its leaders not with suspicion or disdain, but with respect). This was the Reformation critique of the papacy, that it had forgotten its role as a servant or a means of blessing to the Church, but had instead become a position of power, or 'tyranny' as Luther put it. More recent popes have thankfully restored the right perspective. As Pope Francis writes:

> The ministerial priesthood is one means employed by Jesus for the service of his people . . . The configuration of the priest to Christ the head – namely, as the principal source of grace – does not imply an exaltation which would set him above others . . . Even when the function of ministerial priesthood is considered 'hier-archical', it must be remembered that 'it is totally ordered to the holiness of Christ's members'.[7]

Leadership is always borrowed, never owned

There is only one true Leader. This is a radical insight that marks off Christian understandings of leadership from almost any other. We have seen how this affects political authority, radically questioning any claim to absolute power, but the same principle carries through into church leadership. The idea that God is king relativizes all human leadership and rule. When we think we own that leadership, that is when it goes bad. Priestly leaders, who know their leadership serves the purpose of the only true High Priest, know that the people they lead are not their own possession, but God's. If you are a priest, the people you lead are his not yours. Your leadership is borrowed, not owned. Priestly leadership understands its authority to be loaned for the purpose of blessing, not owned for the purpose of power.

Leadership requires humility

When I started out on some serious reading for this book, one of the first texts I turned to was John Chrysostom's *Six Books on the*

Priesthood written around AD 390.[8] I was expecting a treatise on the nature of Christian ministry, but instead found a long apologia, addressed to his friend Basil, for Chrysostom's refusal of the call to priesthood. Rather than a text extolling the value of priesthood and outlining its virtues, it was instead a list of reasons why not to become a priest! Now, of course, Chrysostom does reflect on the qualities needed for Christian leadership, and the general tenor of the book can be summed up in these sentences:

> There are many qualities . . . which a priest ought to have. And the first of these is that he must purify his soul entirely of ambition for the office.[9]

> A preacher must train himself above all else to despise praise.[10]

Chrysostom was not alone. For example, Gregory of Nazianzus and St Augustine showed a similar reluctance to undergo ordination. In other words, the one thing you should look for in a potential Christian leader is a desire not to do the job! Correspondingly, the fatal quality for the Christian leader is vanity. Any personal ambition, any longing for reputation, praise or self-focused glory will inevitably lead attention away from the true Leader of the Church, Jesus Christ, and place it on the leader him- or herself. Now, of course, this is a counsel of perfection. It is impossible to purge oneself entirely of ambition and traces of self-worship, yet to the extent that they are present in the life of a priest or Christian leader, they will undermine and corrupt the distinctively Christian character of the leadership that is offered. A fundamental requirement is a desire not to replace Jesus as the true Head of the Church. There is little room for personality cults in the Church of Jesus Christ.

At a tense point in St Paul's second letter to the Corinthian church, when he is facing severe opposition to his style of ministry and needing to assert his own authority over this church that he had himself planted several years before, he makes a remarkable appeal: 'By the humility and gentleness of Christ, I appeal to you' (2 Cor. 10.1). It is in Christ's humility and gentleness that his power lies, and it is in the humility and gentleness of the priestly leader that Christ's own headship over the Church is both reflected and protected.

The passage from 1 Timothy, this text that tells us so much about early Christian approaches to ministry, indicates what to look out for in a potential Christian leader:

> He must not be a recent convert, or he may become conceited and fall under the same judgment as the devil. He must also have a good reputation with outsiders, so that he will not fall into disgrace and into the devil's trap. (1 Tim. 3.6)

Here we find the requirement that such people be fairly experienced Christians, not over-enamoured with themselves. The assumption is that pride or self-regard is rife in the community outside the Church, and 'conceit' is likely to be common in the recently converted. Only after a period of Christian teaching and the exercise of spiritual discipline will such self-centredness (hopefully) be eroded – or at least the community will have the time to discern whether a person is still affected by conceit or not. Again, the point is that conceit, or self-regard, is fatal for Christian leadership. A desire to place self, rather than Christ, at the centre of the stage is the one quality that cannot be tolerated, as it will transgress this central Christian conviction about the Church – that Christ is the true High Priest; he is the only true Leader.

Humility is not a quality normally associated with leadership. A recent *Harvard Business Review* article spoke of the traditional leadership qualities of 'intelligence, toughness, determination, and vision'. It also spoke of newer, softer ones, particularly 'emotional intelligence, which includes self-awareness, self-regulation, motivation, empathy, and social skill'.[11] Nowhere is humility mentioned. But in Christian understandings of leadership it is crucial. Proud leaders will be unable to stop drawing attention to themselves. They will be jealous for the limelight. Humility will enable leaders to get out of the way, happy to allow that limelight to fall on Christ. Pride will want the congregation to admire the priest's sermons, pastoral skill and record at growing successful churches. Humility will be happy to see all this happen but deflect the glory elsewhere. Humility is a vital quality for Christian leadership: 'Who is wise and understanding among you? Let them show it by their good life, by deeds done in the humility that comes from wisdom' (Jas. 3.13).

Now it is always possible to misunderstand humility. There is an assumption that God requires humility of us, either because we are merely creatures (and he is God), or because we are sinful (and he is good). Now these two statements about God are true, but they are not the main reason why humility matters for leadership. Imagine for a moment that we were perfect or uncreated. Would we be justified in being proud of that? No, of course not. The vital clue is this: that Jesus the Son of God, the true High Priest, was neither a creature nor a sinner, but he was still humble. John tells us:

> Jesus knew that the Father had put all things under his power, and that he had come from God and was returning to God; so he got up from the meal, took off his outer clothing, and wrapped a towel round his waist. After that, he poured water into a basin and began to wash his disciples' feet, drying them with the towel that was wrapped round him. (John 13.3)

It was not despite the fact that the Father had put all things under his power, and that he had come from God and was returning to God, but precisely because of these things, that he washed the feet of his disciples in humble service. It is ultimately because Jesus Christ is humble that Christian leaders are to be humble. If they are not, they will be unable to be images, bearing witness to him, and will instead draw attention away from Christ the true Head of the Church on to themselves.

The burden of the charge made against Paul in 2 Corinthians was that he was somewhat unimpressive, working as he did as a common artisan leather-worker in the shops of Corinth, rather than attaching himself to a wealthy patron as most wandering sophists would have done at the time.[12] He boasts of his 'thorn in

[the] flesh', precisely because it has kept him from being 'conceited' (2 Cor. 12.7). The word used here is *huperairō* – to 'lord it over' people. Again, the one dread Paul has in his understanding of Christian ministry is of a domineering, lordly form of leadership, because it will detract from the true Lord of all. Paul famously boasts not of his impressive CV or résumé, his leadership qualifications, but instead of his sufferings, the number of times he has been beaten, whipped, shipwrecked, gone without sleep or food: in other words, his weakness not his strength. The point of all this is, of course, that his sufferings qualify him as someone worthy of imitation and respect as a Christian leader precisely because they are the mark of Christ: the one who lays down his life as the High Priest of our confession, the one who gives himself up to death so that others might live.

Priestly leaders are always more worried about what people think of Christ than what people think of them. The overall picture is of a leadership style that refuses to take centre stage, but insists on Christ being the centre of attention. The primary quality of the leader is that of Christ-like character, not because that is most effective, but because it serves as a reminder of who really is in charge in the Church: the one who alone intercedes for us at the right hand of the Father, the one who is the head of the body, the Church, the one in whom God's blessings are made available to us, the one who alone can perfect us and bring to the Father.

Leadership creates space for people to flourish

So if the early Christians were adamant that no one could take the place of Christ, and that some of the language used for leadership in their own culture was dangerous, what language did they use? And what does that language tell us about the nature of Christian leadership?

Basil the Great, the Bishop of Caesarea, in what we now know of as Turkey, was one of the most influential Christian leaders in the eastern half of the emerging Byzantine empire towards the end of the fourth century. He wrote frequently about leadership in the Church, often using the phrase 'leaders of the word' to describe church leaders. At one point he writes this:

> What manner of men does Scripture wish those to be who are entrusted with the proclamation of the gospel? . . . as shepherds of the sheep of Christ, not even shrinking from laying down their lives for their sakes on occasion, that they may impart them the gospel of God; as doctors, with much compassion by their knowledge of the teaching of the Lord healing the diseases of souls, to win for them health in Christ and perseverance; as fathers and nurses of their own children, in the great affection of their love in Christ willing to render to them not only the gospel of God but even their own souls . . . as planters of God's branches, inserting nothing that is alien to the vine which is Christ, or that fails to bear fruit, but improving with all diligence such as belong to Him and are fruitful; as builders of God's temple, shaping the soul of each one so that he fits harmoniously onto the foundation of the apostles and prophets.[13]

Basil uses a number of suggestive metaphors for Christian leaders: that of shepherds, doctors, parents, gardeners and construction workers. Most of these are biblical terms, and they are each suggestive of how Christian ministry works.

Take, for example, the image of 'fathers and nurses of their own children', in other words, parents. The New Testament epistles regularly provide lists of qualities of Christian leaders. The first letter of Timothy has the same image:

> Now the overseer is to be above reproach, faithful to his wife, temperate, self-controlled, respectable, hospitable, able to teach, not given to drunkenness, not violent but gentle, not quarrelsome, not a lover of money. He must manage his own family well and see that his children obey him, and he must do so in a manner worthy of full respect. (If anyone does not know how to manage his own family, how can he take care of God's church?)
>
> (1 Tim. 3.2–5)

Here is the requirement that this person is able to 'manage' (the verb is *prohistēmi*) his household well. This idea occurs quite often – the importance of household management is emphasized in 1 Timothy 5.8, 16, and also in Titus 1.6. Why is this such an important factor? The clue is in the statement: 'If anyone does not know how to manage his own family, how can he take care of God's church?' In trying to discern whether someone would make a good priest, a good test is how they operate within their own family, because church leadership is all about building healthy community life, and families or households were (and often still are) the main small communities in which people lived. If a person is able to build good community life in his or her own family, creating a space where family members are not criticized, domineered or indulged, but nurtured and protected, a place where they can find encouragement, where they can manage their dis-agreements well and without rancour, where they want to return again and again, then that is quite a good indication that that person might be good at leading a church. The point is that the qualities of the church leader are akin to those required in families. Anyone who knows anything about family dynamics knows that aggressive, domineering fathers (or mothers for that matter), who require everything to work around them and for their benefit, will never foster healthy family life. The head of the household (usually the father in the first century) has to be someone whose whole focus is the health of the whole group, not any one individual.

A family is a small community the goal of which is the mutual flourishing of its members. In good, healthy families, the head of the family (in many cultures this might be the father, in others the mother, in others both parents) does not dominate or demand, but instead creates good healthy space in which children, spouses, extended family and friends can all grow up into adult, mature, wise human beings. The parent does not force the growth of the child. He or she encourages it, by offering direction, advice, a shoulder to cry on when needed and discipline when appropriate. The child's growth into adulthood is facilitated, not forced.

Likewise, the priestly role of leadership does not force growth, but is deeply aware that the Holy Spirit is the one who brings growth, that Jesus Christ is the shape into which the Church and its members are invited to grow, that maturity happens when people are enabled to 'grow to become in every respect the mature body of him who is the head, that is, Christ' (Eph. 4.15). It creates the space where the community can grow into a body capable of mediating Christ's presence in the world, and bringing healing to a broken and hurting humanity.

This metaphor of the family or household shows how the priestly leader's primary job is to facilitate the health and growth of his or her congregation. Just as the primary requirement for good parents is a devotion to the health of their children and a passion to see them grow into healthy, mature adults, so the primary requirement for the priestly leader is a devotion and desire for the spiritual maturity of the Church and its people, a longing to see them moulded by the Holy Spirit into the image of Jesus Christ, to see the body conformed to its Head.

Basil also uses the image of a gardener (or, in his fourth-century context, a vine dresser). This is an image St Paul uses in writing to the church in Corinth:

> I planted the seed, Apollos watered it, but God has been making it grow. So neither the one who plants nor the one who waters is anything, but only God, who makes things grow. The one who plants and the one who waters have one purpose, and they will each be rewarded according to their own labour. For we are fellow workers in God's service; you are God's field, God's building.
>
> (1 Cor. 3.6–9)

The point is, of course, that gardeners put in place all the conditions for growth, making sure the soil is fertile and properly watered, that the plant is in the sun, and that (in Basil's image) anything added to the plant or the soil does not damage it and ensures its fruitfulness. But they cannot make the plant grow. They can simply provide the conditions in which it can grow. This is their job. It is not up to them to make the plant grow – that is out of their hands and can only happen through the interaction of the plant with the sun and the soil.

Basil's other images point in the same direction. Doctors cannot make a patient healthy. They can only apply medicine, ensure wounds are cleaned and recommend a healthy diet. Shepherds can lead their flock to good pasture and protect it from wolves, but they cannot give it health and make it fat. The image of builders that Basil uses assumes the foundation of the building is already laid, that the architect's plans are in place. The builder merely has to 'shape the soul of each one so that he fits harmoniously onto the foundation of the apostles and prophets'.

In each of these images, the idea of co-operation is present. Here is the notion of Christian leadership as participation in a whole other process and power that lies beyond the capacity of the leaders themselves. Priestly leaders only ever share in some minor way in the priestly leadership of Christ, ensuring that people and churches are put in the right place and given the right conditions for growth, just as a gardener puts the plant in the sun, waters and feeds it, and lets the mysterious powers of growth do the rest. Priestly leadership never usurps or replaces the priestly ministry of Christ. It simply facilitates it, being a means through which Christ does his work of presenting the Church as a perfect offering to the Father.

Epilogue
The widening circle

We have reached the end of our journey. It has been a grand and ambitious one, taking in the beginning and end of the divine plan, the purpose of Creation, the place of humanity, the role of the Church and finally its priestly leaders, all revolving around the centrality of Christ, the one Mediator who stands at the beginning, at the centre and at the end.

Yet, it might still be asked, is this scheme found anywhere explicitly in the pages of Scripture? The Bible has been the main guide for our journey, starting with the letter to the Hebrews and taking in many other places along the way. Yet can this pattern of the priesthood as the means of divine blessing be found explained in discrete parts of the Bible? My answer is yes, and as this book comes to a close, I want to point out just one.

Psalm 67

Psalm 67 has often been seen as a song that fits into the harvest festival celebrations of ancient Israel. The tenses of the text are difficult to determine, so that it could be either a thanksgiving for God's blessing, or a prayer for his blessing. Either way, the theme is divine blessing, and the way in which it comes:

> May God be gracious to us and bless us
>> and make his face shine on us –
>> so that your ways may be known on earth,
>> your salvation among all nations.
> May the peoples praise you, God;
>> may all the peoples praise you.

May the nations be glad and sing for joy,
> for you rule the peoples with equity
> and guide the nations of the earth.
May the peoples praise you, God;
> may all the peoples praise you.
The land yields its harvest;
> God, our God, blesses us.
May God bless us still,
> so that all the ends of the earth will fear him.

The psalm begins and ends with the same note – its chiastic structure starts with a prayer for blessing, and ends with the confirmation
of that blessing. It is also a psalm of joy. It has repeated notes of
praise, gladness and joy, reminding us of the purpose of Creation:
to bring joy both to God and its inhabitants.

Understanding this psalm requires starting with the psalmist
himself. Many commentators have noted that this poem, especially
its first two verses, explicitly refers to the Aaronic priestly blessing
of Numbers 6.24–26: 'The LORD bless you and keep you; the LORD
make his face shine on you and be gracious to you; the LORD turn
his face towards you and give you peace.' In other words, this is
an expansion, meditation on, or elaboration of the priestly blessing that stands at the heart of the life of the people of God. This
is therefore a kind of priestly blessing. These are words that explain
the meaning and fuller content of what the priest means when
he utters the blessing that the face of God will turn towards Israel
and give them peace. In fact the psalm could be seen as recited
by the priest in the Temple itself. One recent commentator says:
'it is plausible to think of a priest leading a congregation in a
prayer for blessing which will bring forth praise and reverence
for Yahweh from the peoples of the world'.[1] The psalm begins with
the priestly leader of the people of God, pronouncing and describing the blessing God gives to the world.

This priestly theology of blessing starts with a prayer for God's
favour upon his people Israel: 'God be gracious to us and bless
us, and make his face shine upon us.' Now this might be seen

as a form of prosperity teaching, especially if we glance forward
to the end of the psalm, to see mention of the land yielding its
harvest, or a form of ethnic nationalism, asking for God's blessing
on Israel alone so it can be seen as the queen among the nations,
the privileged chosen ones. These readings are guilty of moving
too quickly: they chase too fast to the end, without stopping to
see the shape of the whole story. In any case, the priest takes the
role of asking for (or declaring) blessing on God's chosen people,
so they can be what they were always intended to be: the ones on
whom God's face shines.

This psalmist knows that divine blessing on his people, however, is only part of the story. He asks God to bless Israel, not just
for Israel's own sake, but precisely so that 'your ways may be known
on earth, your salvation among all nations'. Already we have moved
quite quickly from the priest, to the people of God, and now to
the nations. The purpose of the divine blessing on his chosen
people is so that, in turn, the peoples of the earth might also praise
God and 'be glad and sing for joy'. God chooses a people and
blesses them so they can be the means through which the whole
human race, the nations that surround Israel, might know the
joy and gladness of divine favour. Furthermore, a specific reason
is given for the nations turning to God in this loud blast of praise:
because God 'rule[s] the people with equity and guide[s] the nations
of the earth'. Israel, the chosen people of God, is to be blessed
so that God's just rule over the world can be both recognized and
established, and his divine governance which directs the overall
course of history – despite its twists and turns, tragedies and
delights – might be revealed. And when they are, the peoples will
in turn join in the song of praise to God, the song of harmony
when the nations unite in praise to their maker.

And yet there is more. When the 'peoples praise you' (v. 5),
the earth itself 'yields its harvest'. The result of the nations being
brought to the praise of God is felt even in the soil, the dirt of
the earth itself. The earth becomes fruitful, supporting life, giving
joy, just as it was always meant to. Even the inanimate Creation

joins in the song, becoming fruitful and sustaining life in the way it was always meant to.

The psalm comes to its triumphant conclusion in the final note of the praise of God. As the land brings forth fruit, it provokes thanksgiving for divine blessing. And when that blessing comes, the world lives in harmony, with the whole earth (or literally 'the ends of the earth') respecting, worshipping, united in praise of God the Creator. The produce of the earth is not an end in itself, but is a means to the praise of God and the joy of Creation.[2] Derek Kidner entitles this psalm 'The Spreading Circle', and it's not hard to see what he means: here is the spreading circle of God's blessing from the Church, to the nations, to the whole earth itself.[3]

What is not yet in sight is the precise shape of this blessing in Christ-like form. The New Testament will fill out both the form which this redeemed humanity will take in Christ, and the hard-won cost of this harmony to God. This is a psalm which does not really deal with the realities of a broken, sinful world, and its need for redemption and healing as well as for fulfilment. Nonetheless, even with its incomplete nature, here we see the whole divine plan of blessing outlined, even in reverse: God uses priests to bless his chosen people, who are to turn the nations to the praise of God so that in turn, the earth itself is brought to fruitfulness, to the praise of God and the joy of both Creator and Creation.

Summary

To draw things to a close, let me spell out what I think some the key implications of the approach taken by this book are for us today – in other words, the good news that a healthy theology of priesthood declares.

- God's desire is to bless his Creation and to bring it to its fulfilment. He does that through Christ, the one Mediator between God and Creation. And yet he chooses to involve us in various ways in that priestly blessing. That is our privilege, as human beings, as the Church, or as priests.

- We human beings are fully part of the rest of Creation, not exalted above it. Richard Bauckham speaks of the 'fellowship of creation', and he is quite right: rather than being superior, separate from and dominant over the rest of Creation, a proper theology of our priestly role within Creation tells us we are fully part of it, sharing in its nature and, to a certain extent, its fate. As St Francis saw so clearly, the sun, moon, water, air and fire, not to mention the animals themselves, are our brothers and sisters, not our servants.

- We humans stand under a divine calling. We may be part of Creation, but we are graced with a special responsibility to care for that Creation, developing it and protecting it from harm. This brings responsibility but also dignity, as it is a calling that rests on every human being, not just its political leaders. Each one of us is given a small part of Creation, be that a school, a business, a family, a garden, a bedroom even, to nurture and protect just as Christ himself would.

- The Church is fully part of the rest of humanity, not better or separate, exalted above everyone else. Being called by God to be a priestly people does not make Christians any less a part of the rest of humanity, subject to the same impulses, desires, struggles and joys. This again is a relief, making us a little more patient with our fellow Christians, but also enabling us to reach across to other people, not down to them. Christians have more in common with non-Christians than we sometimes like to think!

- The Church's primary calling is directed towards people, drawing people back into fellowship with God through Christ, in its evangelism, compassion and worship. It makes the Church's role a little more manageable. It is not primarily the Church's calling to care for Creation: that is the human calling. It is not the Church's job to produce the best music, art, science or literature: that is the human vocation, not just the Christian one. We need not get too distressed if some of the best art or science happens outside the Church. As Church we do our bit, but we rejoice every time technology produces useful things, flood defences are raised and laws are passed that protect green fields or rain forests. It is the Church's task to join in Christ's praise of the Father on behalf of the rest of humanity, to urge the friends and family we have to be reconciled to God, and to demonstrate what it means to live a fully and richly human life.

- The primary identity of priests is as baptized Christians, deeply identified with the Church and its members. They are lay before they are leaders. They are part of a priestly people, called to serve those very people and do whatever it takes to ensure their maturity in Christ. They are priestly, not in any sense exalted over the Christian community, but called to bring it the divine blessing so that it can be perfected and offered to God as an act of worship.
- Priests are here to serve the Church, to bless the Church, and to enable it to glorify Christ its true Head. They might like to focus directly on political activism or Creation care, but their primary role is to develop a community of Christians who are themselves politically active and doing what they can to care for their part of Creation. Priests are not meant to bypass the Church, but enable the Church to be itself.
- The purpose of Creation is joy. In a world where we are often made to feel that the purpose of life is work, production, success, wealth or a host of other things, to be reminded that we are here in the fullest sense to enjoy God, ourselves and the Creation is a huge relief, and a reminder that our selves are to be enjoyed in Christ, not to be taken too seriously. We are here for the glory of God, which shines most clearly when we enjoy him and his Creation to the full.

Notes

Introduction

1 A classic example is E. O. James, *The Nature and Function of Priesthood* (London: Thames & Hudson, 1961).

2 See L. Newbigin, *The Gospel in a Pluralist Society* (London: SPCK, 1989), ch. 7, 'The Logic of Election', for a stimulating discussion of this point.

3 M. Scarlata, *Am I My Brother's Keeper? Christian Citizenship in a Globalized Society* (Eugene, OR: Wipf and Stock, 2013) is an excellent modern discussion of the Cain and Abel story and its application today. It sees Cain and Abel as moral types, offering two ways of responding to God rather than explaining God's favour on Abel because he was 'good', or his judgement on Abel because he was 'bad'.

4 J. Calvin, *Institutes of the Christian Religion* (Philadelphia, PA: Westminster Press, 1960), III.23.4–5.

5 K. Barth, *Church Dogmatics* (London: T&T Clark, 2009), II.2.99.

6 Barth, *Church Dogmatics*, II.2.146.

7 Barth, *Church Dogmatics*, II.2.103.

8 R. E. Brian, *Covering Up Luther: How Barth's Christology Challenged the* Deus Absconditus *that Haunts Modernity* (Eugene, OR: Wipf and Stock, 2013) is an interesting exercise in how Barth's Christology gives content to the choice of God in Christ, emphasizing the fullness of God's presence in Christ, rather than the more disturbing implications of the hidden God of some aspects of Reformation theology.

9 F. L. Battles, 'God was Accommodating Himself to Human Capacity', *Interpretation* 31 (1977), 19–38.

1 The priesthood of Christ: descent

1 The question of the addressees of the letter remains a moot point. The title 'To the Hebrews' was only given to the letter in the second century, so does not indicate any privileged insight into the original recipients. Most commentators have assumed a Jewish Christian audience, for example, more recently, D. A. DeSilva, *Perseverance in*

159

Gratitude: A Socio-Rhetorical Commentary on the Epistle "to the Hebrews" (Grand Rapids, MI: Eerdmans, 2000), who suggests it was written after AD 70 to those nostalgic for the Jerusalem Temple. Others argue for a mixed audience (e.g. C. R. Koester, *Hebrews: A New Translation, with Introduction and Commentary* (New Haven, CT: Yale University Press, 2001)). Either way, the author presumably had in mind at least some Jewish Christians as those who were to be its first readers.

2 The date of the epistle is debated, but it is mostly thought to have been written before the destruction of the Jerusalem Temple in AD 70, due to the absence of any reference to that event (*pace* DeSilva above) and to its references to persecution.

3 This, as Colin Gunton has pointed out, preserves the sense that God is both related to his Creation, yet remains distinct from it, avoiding the twin dangers of idealism (that the world is merely a projection of our minds) and pantheism (that the world is merely a projection of God's being or mind). C. Gunton, *Christ and Creation* (Eugene, OR: Wipf and Stock, 1992), pp. 75–77.

4 Hebrews does not really have a *Logos* Christology of this kind – the use of '*Logos*' in Hebrews is usually a reference to the message of the gospel (e.g. 5.12; 12.5). The only exception to this is the implication in 1.2 which asserts that God has 'spoken to us by his Son'.

5 Although not a particularly strong theme in the letter to the Hebrews, this draws in the Trinitarian nature of a proper theology of Creation, in that the Holy Spirit is the one who brings created things to their proper fulfilment, as an *arrabōn*, or down payment of the future (2 Cor. 1.22; 5.5).

6 K. Barth, *Church Dogmatics* (London: T&T Clark, 2009), II.2.1.

7 It is worth noting, however, that recent scholarship on Gnosticism implies a less dualistic and docetic view of salvation than Patristic opponents of Gnosticism such as Irenaeus, Hippolytus and Tertullian imply. See S. Pétrement, *A Separate God: The Christian Origins of Gnosticism* (San Francisco, CA: Harper & Row, 1990); A. H. B. Logan, *Gnostic Truth and Christian Heresy: A Study in the History of Gnosticism* (Edinburgh: T&T Clark, 1996).

8 Colin Gunton argues that this idea of the 'Forms' as a mediating factor between God and Creation was smuggled into Christian theology, notably by Augustine (see C. Gunton, *A Brief Theology*

of Revelation (Edinburgh: T&T Clark, 1995), ch. 2 for a brief summary of his argument). Gunton's critique of Augustine has recently been challenged in B. G. Green, *Colin Gunton and the Failure of Augustine: The Theology of Colin Gunton in Light of Augustine* (Eugene, OR: Wipf and Stock, 2011).

9 A useful summary of the debate over Eutyches' Christology is found in H. Chadwick, *The Church in Ancient Society: From Galilee to Gregory the Great* (Oxford: Oxford University Press, 2001), pp. 551–6.

10 Most orthodox Christologies hold that Christ assumed sinful, not sinless, human nature, so that his identification with us is complete, yet because of his obedience to the Father, he did not actually commit sin. See, for example, T. F. Torrance, *The Mediation of Christ* (Exeter: Paternoster Press, 1983), p. 74.

11 This is a point brought out very well by Marcus Plested's chapter on Eutychianism in B. Quash and M. Ward, *Heresies and How to Avoid Them* (London: SPCK, 2007).

12 Luther writes of 'Christ, our Priest, in whose humanity alone we are protected and saved'. *Luther's Works*, ed. J. Pelikan et al., 55 vols (St Louis, MO: Concordia Publishing House, 1955–), XXIX.167.

13 See Torrance, *The Mediation of Christ*, ch. 3.

14 For discussion of this point, see W. Pannenberg, *Jesus – God and Man* (London: SCM Press, 1968), ch. 6.

15 J. Calvin, *Institutes of the Christian Religion* (Philadelphia, PA: Westminster Press, 1960), II.12.2.

16 Calvin, *Institutes*, II.12.1.

17 Calvin, *Institutes*, III.2.4.

18 For the development of this idea, see G. Tomlin, *The Prodigal Spirit: The Trinity, the Church and the Future of the World* (London: Alpha International, 2011).

19 See J. T. Billings, *Calvin, Participation and the Gift: The Activity of Believers in Union with Christ* (Oxford: Oxford University Press, 2007), ch. 2.

20 Calvin links our adoption as sons to Christ's natural sonship: 'men ... become God's sons by free adoption because Christ is the Son of God by nature'. *Institutes*, II.14.5.

21 Athanasius, *De Incarnatione Verbi Dei*, 14.1–2.

22 Torrance, *The Mediation of Christ*, p. 67.

23 The phrase occurs in the *Loci Communes Theologici*: W. Pauck, ed., *Melanchthon and Bucer*, Library of Christian Classics (Philadelphia, PA: Westminster Press, 1969), p. 21. In its context, Melanchthon is simply making an anti-speculative point, that we know Christ from what he does, rather than knowing him in his inner nature, but it can be misunderstood as distancing us from Christ.

24 This would certainly be a misunderstanding of Luther, who makes it clear that the righteousness that justification brings is Christ's own righteousness which becomes ours by faith. See, for example, in Luther's *The Freedom of a Christian* of 1525: 'Here we have a most pleasing vision not only of communion but of a blessed struggle and victory and salvation and redemption. Christ is God and man in one person. He has neither sinned nor died, and is not condemned, and he cannot sin, die, or be condemned; his righteousness, life, and salvation are unconquerable, eternal, omnipotent. By the wedding ring of faith he shares in the sins, death, and pains of hell which are his bride's. As a matter of fact, he makes them his own and acts as if they were his own and as if he himself had sinned; he suffered, died, and descended into hell that he might overcome them all. Now since it was such a one who did all this, and death and hell could not swallow him up, these were necessarily swallowed up by him in a mighty duel; for his righteousness is greater than the sins of all men, his life stronger than death, his salvation more invincible than hell. Thus the believing soul by means of the pledge of its faith is free in Christ, its bridegroom, free from all sins, secure against death and hell, and is endowed with the eternal righteousness, life, and salvation of Christ its bridegroom.' *Luther's Works*, XXXI.351.

25 Interestingly, Thomas Aquinas does not see it this way: he implies Christ is more of an intermediary than a mediator, standing between humanity and God, rather than uniting them and enabling true participation, which is why he sees Christ's mediation only in his human rather than his divine nature: 'We may consider two things in a mediator: first, that he is a mean; secondly, that he unites others. Now it is of the nature of a mean to be distant from each extreme: while it unites by communicating to one that which belongs to the other. Now neither of these can be applied to Christ as God, but only

as man. For, as God, He does not differ from the Father and the Holy Ghost in nature and power of dominion: nor have the Father and the Holy Ghost anything that the Son has not, so that He be able to communicate to others something belonging to the Father or the Holy Ghost, as though it were belonging to others than Himself. But both can be applied to Him as man. Because, as man, He is distant both from God, by nature, and from man by dignity of both grace and glory. Again, it belongs to Him, as man, to unite men to God, by communicating to men both precepts and gifts, and by offering satisfaction and prayers to God for men. And therefore He is most truly called Mediator, as man.' Aquinas, *Summa Theologica*, III.q26.

26 Athanasius, *De Incarnatione Verbi Dei*, 9.3.

2 The priesthood of Christ: ascent

1 I take it that the Son would have become incarnate even if the world had not fallen, as Creation was made in and for him. However, that entry into Creation would not have involved the cross had the world not fallen. This is the 'supralapsarian' view in a long-standing debate in both medieval and Reformation theology. For further discussion, see: M. M. Adams, *Christ and Horrors: The Coherence of Christology* (Cambridge: Cambridge University Press, 2006); E. C. van Driel, *Incarnation Anyway: Arguments for Supralapsarian Christology* (Oxford: Oxford University Press, 2008); O. Crisp, *Revisioning Christology: Theology in the Reformed Tradition* (Farnham: Ashgate, 2011), ch. 2.

2 See also 9.14; 10.2, 22.

3 John Davies' book on Old Testament priesthood uses this very word to describe the priest: 'The priest functioned as an intermediary between God and people. This is most clearly shown in his role as one who declares or imparts divine blessing and as one who intercedes with God on behalf of the people.' J. A. Davies, *A Royal Priesthood: Literary and Intertextual Perspectives on an Image of Israel in Exodus 19.6* (London: T&T Clark International, 2004), p. 163.

4 'The priest belongs in two worlds. While his everyday life is among his fellow Israelites, when he dons his vestments and crosses the threshold, he becomes a participant in the heavenly or ideal world.' Davies, *Royal Priesthood*, p. 164.

5 C. Gunton, *Christ and Creation* (Eugene, OR: Wipf and Stock, 1992), p. 58.

6 'In short, his suffering, death and exaltation formed the defining moment of Christ's priesthood. But that priesthood embraced his whole story, and not least the years about which we know most: his public priestly ministry, when he obediently gave himself totally to the service of the kingdom. The earthly and heavenly priesthood of Christ may be distinguished, but belong inseparably together.' G. O'Collins and M. K. Jones, *Jesus our Priest: A Christian Approach to the Priesthood of Christ* (Oxford: Oxford University Press, 2010), p. 61.

7 Athanasius, *Contra Arianos*, 2.8.

8 J. Calvin, *Institutes of the Christian Religion* (Philadelphia, PA: Westminster Press, 1960), II.16.5.

9 See Leviticus 7 for examples of the different kinds of sacrifice in the Old Testament.

10 There are references to the resurrection of individual people such as Isaac (11.19 – see also 11.35). Hebrews 13.20, with its reference to 'the God of peace who . . . brought back from the dead our Lord Jesus' (and possibly 6.2), is the only clear reference to the resurrection of Christ himself. The epistle does not focus on the resurrection, but rather 'presupposes' the traditions of resurrection in the Pauline writings. See C. R. Koester, *Hebrews: A New Translation, with Introduction and Commentary* (New Haven, CT: Yale University Press, 2001), p. 491.

11 D. Moffitt, '"If Another Priest Arises": Jesus' Resurrection and the High Priestly Christology of Hebrews', in *A Cloud of Witnesses: The Theology of Hebrews in its Ancient Contexts*, ed. R. Bauckham, T. Hart, N. McDonald and D. Driver (London: T&T Clark, 2008), pp. 68–79.

12 W. Pannenberg, *Jesus – God and Man* (London: SCM Press, 1968), p. 363.

13 Pannenberg, *Jesus – God and Man*, p. 224.

14 To use a perhaps unlikely example, it is a little like a football team that wins the Champions League and thus goes down in history as a great team, the best of the year. Until that point, it would be impossible to tell whether it was truly a great team – a team that loses the final is still the same team as it was all season, but it is the winning of the trophy that establishes that team as great and memorable. In

the light of that victory the story of the season is retold as a story of triumph, of progress towards glory, rather than that of a team that strove for glory but failed to reach it. After its confirmation as the Champions, it is always looked back on as a great team, even in the retelling of the story of the season. In the same way, Jesus' true glory, greatness and identity is revealed and established at the resurrection.

15 As Pannenberg's Christology always begins 'from below', he considers that of the three traditional 'offices' of Christ, only the prophetic office, rather than the kingly or priestly ones can be taken as read from the historical Jesus: 'While we would rather not speak of a priestly office of Jesus, we do not deny that through his fate Jesus took the place occupied in Israel and other religions by the priesthood and the sacrificial rituals.' Pannenberg, *Jesus – God and Man*, p. 221.

16 D. Farrow, *Ascension Theology* (London: T&T Clark International, 2011), p. 44. See also D. Farrow, *Ascension and Ecclesia: On the Significance of the Doctrine of the Ascension for Ecclesiology and Christian Cosmology* (Edinburgh: T&T Clark, 1999).

17 See G. Tomlin, *The Prodigal Spirit: The Trinity, the Church and the Future of the World* (London: Alpha International, 2011), ch. 2.

18 St Basil the Great, *On the Holy Spirit* (Crestwood, NY: St Vladimir's Seminary Press, 1980), p. 62.

19 Gunton, *Christ and Creation*, p. 57.

20 J. Calvin, *Hebrews and 1&2 Peter* (Grand Rapids, MI: Eerdmans, 1963), p. 59.

21 See J. Torrance, *Worship, Community, and the Triune God of Grace* (Carlisle: Paternoster Press, 1996) for an excellent explanation of this point.

22 This is my translation of the Greek word *metathesis* which occurs at this point.

23 Pannenberg, *Jesus – God and Man*, p. 369.

3 Priesthood questioned

1 1 Clement 40.

2 Augustine, *City of God*, 20.10.

3 See Paul Philibert, 'Issues for a Theology of Priesthood', in *The Theology of Priesthood*, ed. D. J. Goergen and A. Garrido (Collegeville, MN: Michael Glazier, 2000), pp. 15–16.

4 St John Chrysostom, *Six Books on the Priesthood* (Crestwood, NY: St Vladimir's Seminary Press, 1984).

5 G. O'Collins and M. K. Jones, *Jesus our Priest: A Christian Approach to the Priesthood of Christ* (Oxford: Oxford University Press, 2010), pp. 125–6.

6 See R. N. Swanson, *Religion and Devotion in Europe c.1215–c.1515* (Cambridge: Cambridge University Press, 1995), pp. 236–41.

7 *Luther's Works*, ed. J. Pelikan et al., 55 vols (St Louis, MO: Concordia Publishing House, 1955–), XLIV.127.

8 *Luther's Works*, XLIV.129.

9 *Luther's Works*, XLIV.20.

10 *Luther's Works*, XLIV.14.

11 *Luther's Works*, XLIV.19.

12 *Luther's Works*, XLIV.34.

13 *Luther's Works*, XLIV.35.

14 See the historical detective work conducted by J. T. Wengert, *Priesthood, Pastors, Bishops: Public Ministry for the Reformation and Today* (Minneapolis, MN: Fortress Press, 2008), pp. 1–4.

15 Wengert, *Priesthood, Pastors, Bishops*, p. 12.

16 For a useful discussion of Luther on priesthood, see B. A. Gerrish, 'Priesthood and Ministry: Luther's Fifth Means of Grace', in *The Old Protestantism and the New: Essays on the Reformation Heritage* (Edinburgh: T&T Clark, 1982), pp. 90–105.

17 J. Calvin, *Calvin: Theological Treatises*, ed. and trans. by J. K. S. Reid (Philadelphia, PA: Westminster Press, 1954), p. 95.

18 J. Calvin, *Institutes of the Christian Religion* (Philadelphia, PA: Westminster Press, 1960), IV.7.21.

19 Calvin, *Institutes*, IV.6.2.

20 *Calvin: Theological Treatises*, p. 157.

21 *Calvin: Theological Treatises*, p. 155.

22 *Calvin: Theological Treatises*, p. 156.

23 *Calvin: Theological Treatises*, p. 156.

24 Calvin, *Institutes*, IV.19.28.

25 This spirit was particularly strong in the various revolutions in religion and politics that took place in the seventeenth century, where it is hard sometimes to see what is chicken and what is egg – did a revolt against clerical priesthood lead to the egalitarian

political visions of the English Civil War, for example, or vice versa?

26 W. H. Lazareth, *Christians in Society: Luther, the Bible, and Social Ethics* (Minneapolis, MN: Fortress Press, 2001), p. 217.

27 *Luther's Works*, LII.39.

28 *Luther's Works*, XXXVII.95.

29 E. Brunner, *The Mediator: A Study of the Central Doctrine of the Christian Faith* (London: Lutterworth Press, 1934), p. 274.

30 See in particular, J. T. Billings, *Calvin, Participation and the Gift: The Activity of Believers in Union with Christ* (Oxford: Oxford University Press, 2007); J. Canlis, *Calvin's Ladder: A Spiritual Theology of Ascent and Ascension* (Grand Rapids, MI: Eerdmans, 2010).

31 See G. Tomlin, *The Prodigal Spirit: The Trinity, the Church and the Future of the World* (London: Alpha International, 2011), ch. 1 for an exposition of this theme.

32 Billings, *Calvin, Participation and the Gift*, p. 82.

33 Canlis, *Calvin's Ladder*, ch. 2.

34 Canlis, *Calvin's Ladder*, p. 237.

35 Calvin, *Institutes*, II.15.3.

4 The priesthood of humanity

1 R. Bauckham, *The Bible and Ecology* (London: DLT, 2010), p. 79.

2 An excellent exploration of the place of joy and happiness in Christian theology is: E. T. Charry, *God and the Art of Happiness* (Grand Rapids, MI: Eerdmans, 2010).

3 St Basil the Great, *On the Human Condition* (Crestwood, NY: St Vladimir's Seminary Press, 2005): see the 'Second Homily on the Origin of Humanity'. Jürgen Moltmann also suggests that the word 'image' implies 'outward representation', or the idea that humanity represents God within Creation. On the other hand, the word 'likeness' refers to the 'inward relationship', the idea of reflecting God's nature. J. Moltmann, *God in Creation: An Ecological Doctrine of Creation* (London: SCM Press, 1985), pp. 218–19.

4 C. Gunton, *Christ and Creation* (Eugene, OR: Wipf and Stock, 1992), p. 121.

5 For example, John Zizioulas emphasizes the element of *Anaphora*, or lifting up of the elements, as the human action of offering Creation back to God in expectation of the Holy Spirit's corresponding descent

upon those elements. J. Zizioulas, 'Priest of Creation', in *Environmental Stewardship: Critical Perspectives – Past and Present*, ed. R. J. Berry (London: T&T Clark, 2006), pp. 273–90 (pp. 280–1).

6 As we noted in Calvin, who sees 'offering' as 'to offer ourselves and ours to God'. J. Calvin, *Institutes of the Christian Religion* (Philadelphia, PA: Westminster Press, 1960), IV.19.28.

7 This is the language used for the Philippians' monetary gift to Paul referred to in Philippians 4.18.

8 T. F. Torrance, *Transformation and Convergence in the Frame of Knowledge. Explorations in the Interrelations of Scientific and Theological Enterprise* (Belfast: Christian Journals, 1984), p. 264. See also J. Begbie, *Voicing Creation's Praise: Towards a Theology of the Arts* (London: T&T Clark, 1991).

9 Moltmann, *God in Creation*, p. 71.

10 See for example, L. White, 'The Historical Roots of our Ecological Crisis', *Science* 155 (1967), 1203–7.

11 R. Bauckham, *God and the Crisis of Freedom: Biblical and Contemporary Perspectives* (Louisville, KY: Westminster John Knox Press, 2002), ch. 7, and more extensively in Bauckham, *Bible and Ecology*.

12 Bauckham, *Bible and Ecology*, p. 30.

13 See also R. Bauckham, 'Modern Domination of Nature: Historical Origins and Biblical Critique', in *Environmental Stewardship*, ed. R. J. Berry (London: T&T Clark, 2006), pp. 32–50.

14 Bauckham, *Bible and Ecology*, p. 147.

15 Bauckham, *Bible and Ecology*, p. 114.

16 E. Theokritoff, 'Creation and Priesthood in Modern Orthodox Thinking', *Ecotheology* 10.3 (2005), 344–63.

17 Theokritoff, 'Creation and Priesthood', p. 351.

18 The eschatological direction of Creation is emphasized in Moltmann, *God in Creation*, ch. 8.

5 The priesthood of the Church

1 C. R. Seitz, *Figured Out: Typology and Providence in Christian Scripture* (Louisville, KY: Westminster John Knox Press, 2001), p. 148.

2 J. A. T. Robinson, *On Being the Church in the World* (London: SCM Press, 1960), p. 97.

3 The body of Christ is best seen as metaphor for the same reasons outlined elsewhere in this chapter: it is important to keep the distinction

between Creator and Creation, and to avoid the mistake of identifying the Church with Christ in a full, literal way that could lead to the idolatry of worshipping the Church rather than Christ himself.

4 St Basil the Great, *On the Holy Spirit* (Crestwood, NY: St Vladimir's Seminary Press, 1980), p. 62.

5 J. Torrance, *Worship, Community, and the Triune God of Grace* (Carlisle: Paternoster Press, 1996), p. 84.

6 Karl Barth writes of the Christian at prayer: 'With the whole community, he asks in the name of Jesus, on the basis of his intercession, attaching himself to him, standing at his side. Therefore in his own prayer, he cannot disregard or deny or crowd out the true and proper Subject of prayer who recites the prayer before him.' *Church Dogmatics* (London: T&T Clark, 2009), III.3.280.

7 S. McDonald, *Re-Imaging Election: Divine Election as Representing God to Others and Others to God* (Grand Rapids, MI: Eerdmans, 2010), p. 140.

8 See W. J. Sheils, ed., *The Church and Healing*, Studies in Church History (Oxford: Basil Blackwell, 1982) for evidence of the centrality of this practice in the history of prayer.

9 The language of the death of Christ as a sacrifice is not, of course, restricted to Hebrews. It is also found in Romans 3.25; Ephesians 5.2; 1 John 2.2; 4.10, etc.

10 M. Jinkins, *The Church Faces Death: Ecclesiology in a Post-Modern Context* (Oxford: Oxford University Press, 1999), pp. 27, 32.

11 Torrance, *Worship*, p. 30.

6 The priesthood of ministers

1 This chapter faces a problem of terminology. What name do we give the Church's ordained 'officials' – those the Church sets apart to 'direct the affairs of the church' (1 Tim. 5.17)? The term 'presbyter' could work, but is a particular kind of official and is rather quaint, with not many churches using it. The term 'minister' is not ideal either as, of course, every Christian is in some sense a minister. As I am arguing that there is a priestly character to this role of leadership in the Church, I will mainly use the word 'priest' to describe it.

2 R. C. Moberly, *Ministerial Priesthood* (London: SPCK, 1969).

3 R. Greenwood, *Transforming Priesthood: A New Theology of Mission and Ministry* (London: SPCK, 1994), p. 11.

4 For example, A. Hanson, *Church Sacraments and Ministry* (London: Mowbray, 1975), which argues for a priesthood that represents the Church rather than Christ, a 'ministerial representative priesthood, rather than vicarious, autocratic priesthood' (p. 113).

5 *Baptism, Eucharist and Ministry* (Geneva: World Council of Churches, 1982), pp. 18–19.

6 This is also clear in Luke's version, where the immediate note struck after the baptism is that of the beginning of his public ministry: 'Now Jesus himself was about thirty years old when he began his ministry' (3.23).

7 For example, in Josephus, *Antiquities*, 1.311, and Acts 7.43.

8 St John Chrysostom, *Six Books on the Priesthood* (Crestwood, NY: St Vladimir's Seminary Press, 1984), p. 93.

9 M. Volf, *After Our Likeness: The Church as the Image of the Trinity* (Grand Rapids, MI: Eerdmans, 1998), p. 246. Not everyone will agree with his specifying the *local*, rather than the universal, Church here but his point about ordination *vis-à-vis* the entirety of the Church remains.

10 K. Barth, *Church Dogmatics* (London: T&T Clark, 2009), III.4.104.

11 For further discussion on the relationship between evangelism and friendship, see G. Tomlin, *The Provocative Church* (London: SPCK, 2014).

12 J. Moltmann, *A Broad Place: An Autobiography* (London: SCM Press, 2007), p. 203.

13 J. Calvin, *Institutes of the Christian Religion* (Philadelphia, PA: Westminster Press, 1960), IV.1.9.

14 This is a point emphasized by B. C. Milner, *Calvin's Doctrine of the Church* (Leiden: Brill, 1970), ch. 4.

15 C. Handy, *The Empty Raincoat: Making Sense of the Future* (London: Arrow, 1995).

16 L. Newbigin, *The Household of God* (London: SCM Press, 1957) is a wonderful exploration of these three elements and the necessity of all three: the Protestant emphasis on the Word, the Catholic emphasis on the sacraments and the Pentecostal emphasis on the Spirit in the Church.

17 This problem of the repetitive nature of much Christian ministry is not a new one. Augustine in his *On Catechizing Beginners* writes:

'Now if we find it distasteful to be constantly rehearsing familiar phrases that are suited to the ears of small children, we should draw close to these small children with a brother's love, or a father's or a mother's, and as a result of our empathy with them, the oft-repeated phrases will sound new to us also when our listeners are touched by us as we speak and we are touched by them as they learn, each of us comes to dwell in the other, and so they as it were speak in us what they hear, while we in some way learn in them what we teach' (*De catechizandis rudibus*, 12.17, in W. Harmless, *Augustine and the Catechumenate* (Collegeville, MN: Liturgical Press, 1995).

18 See G. Tomlin, *The Prodigal Spirit: The Trinity, the Church and the Future of the World* (London: Alpha International, 2011), pp. 27–36.

19 R. Allen, *Missionary Methods: St Paul's or Ours?* (Grand Rapids, MI: Eerdmans, 1983).

20 Allen, *Missionary Methods*, pp. i–ii.

7 Priestly leadership

1 For a critique of modern Christian talk of leadership, see J. Lewis-Anthony, *You are the Messiah, and I Should Know: Why Leadership is a Myth (and Probably a Heresy)* (London: Bloomsbury, 2013).

2 For a critique of the classic priest-does-all model, see J. Lewis-Anthony, *If You Meet George Herbert on the Road, Kill Him: Radically Re-thinking Priestly Ministry* (London: Continuum, 2009). He proposes a model of the priest as Watchman, Witness and Weaver, and posits the need for a clear sense of rule, role, responsibility, reckoning and reconciling. And presumably a gift for alliteration.

3 *Archontōn tou aiōvos.*

4 *Archonti tōv daimoniōn*: Matt. 9.34; 12.24; Mark 3.22; Luke 11.15.

5 Even the Psalms that celebrate Israelite kingship still draw attention to the ultimate kingship of God, for example: 'For God is the King of all the earth; sing to him a psalm of praise. God reigns over the nations; God is seated on his holy throne' (Ps. 47.7–8).

6 W. Pannenberg, *Jesus – God and Man* (London: SCM Press, 1968), p. 365.

7 Pope Francis, *Apostolic Exhortation: Evangelii Gaudium* (Vatican City: Vatican Press, 2014), p. 104.

8 St John Chrysostom, *Six Books on the Priesthood* (Crestwood, NY: St Vladimir's Seminary Press, 1984).

9 Chrysostom, *Six Books on the Priesthood*, p. 80.

10 Chrysostom, *Six Books on the Priesthood*, p. 133.

11 <http://hbr.org/2004/01/what-makes-a-leader/ar/1>.

12 On patronage in Roman cities such as Corinth, see two articles on the topic in R. Horsley, ed., *Paul and Empire: Religion and Power in Roman Imperial Society* (Harrisburg, PA: Trinity Press International, 1997): P. Garnsey and R. Saller, 'Patronal Power Relations', pp. 96–103; J. K. Chow, 'Patronage in Roman Corinth', pp. 104–25. See also R. F. Hock, 'Paul's Tentmaking and the Problem of his Social Class', *JBL* 97 (1978), 555–64; and R. F. Hock, *The Social Context of Paul's Ministry: Tentmaking and Apostleship* (Philadelphia, PA: Fortress Press, 1980).

13 Quoted in P. J. Fedwick, *The Church and the Charisma of Leadership in Basil of Caesarea* (Toronto: Pontifical Institute of Mediaeval Studies, 1979), pp. 99–100.

Epilogue

1 M. E. Tate, *Psalms 51–150* (Nashville, TN: Thomas Nelson, 2010), p. 155.

2 A. Weiser, *The Psalms: A Commentary* (London: SCM Press, 1962), p. 474.

3 D. Kidner, *Psalms 1–72: An Introduction and Commentary* (Nottingham: Inter-Varsity Press, 1978; repr. 2008), p. 236.

References

Introduction

Battles, F. L., 'God was Accommodating Himself to Human Capacity', *Interpretation* 31 (1977), 19–38.

Brian, R. E., *Covering Up Luther: How Barth's Christology Challenged the* Deus Absconditus *that Haunts Modernity* (Eugene, OR: Wipf and Stock, 2013).

Calvin, J., *Institutes of the Christian Religion* (Philadelphia, PA: Westminster Press, 1960).

James, E. O., *The Nature and Function of Priesthood* (London: Thames & Hudson, 1961).

Newbigin, L., *The Gospel in a Pluralist Society* (London: SPCK, 1989).

Scarlata, M., *Am I My Brother's Keeper? Christian Citizenship in a Globalized Society* (Eugene, OR: Wipf and Stock, 2013).

1 The priesthood of Christ: descent

Barth, K., *Church Dogmatics* (London: T&T Clark, 2009).

Billings, J. T., *Calvin, Participation and the Gift: The Activity of Believers in Union with Christ* (Oxford: Oxford University Press, 2007).

Calvin, J., *Institutes of the Christian Religion* (Philadelphia, PA: Westminster Press, 1960).

Chadwick, H., *The Church in Ancient Society: From Galilee to Gregory the Great* (Oxford: Oxford University Press, 2001).

DeSilva, D. A., *Perseverance in Gratitude: A Socio-Rhetorical Commentary on the Epistle "to the Hebrews"* (Grand Rapids, MI: Eerdmans, 2000).

Green, B. G., *Colin Gunton and the Failure of Augustine: The Theology of Colin Gunton in Light of Augustine* (Eugene, OR: Wipf and Stock, 2011).

Gunton, C., *A Brief Theology of Revelation* (Edinburgh: T&T Clark, 1995).

Gunton, C., *Christ and Creation* (Eugene, OR: Wipf and Stock, 1992).

Koester, C. R., *Hebrews: A New Translation, with Introduction and Commentary* (New Haven, CT: Yale University Press, 2001).

Logan, A. H. B., *Gnostic Truth and Christian Heresy: A Study in the History of Gnosticism* (Edinburgh: T&T Clark, 1996).

Luther, M., *Luther's Works*, ed. J. Pelikan et al., 55 vols (St Louis, MO: Concordia Publishing House, 1955–).

Pannenberg, W., *Jesus – God and Man* (London: SCM Press, 1968).

Pauck, W., ed., *Melanchthon and Bucer*, Library of Christian Classics (Philadelphia, PA: Westminster Press, 1969).

Pétrement, S., *A Separate God: The Christian Origins of Gnosticism* (San Francisco, CA: Harper & Row, 1990).

Quash, B. and M. Ward, *Heresies and How to Avoid Them* (London: SPCK, 2007).

Tomlin, G., *The Prodigal Spirit: The Trinity, the Church and the Future of the World* (London: Alpha International, 2011).

Torrance, T. F., *The Mediation of Christ* (Exeter: Paternoster Press, 1983).

2 The priesthood of Christ: ascent

Adams, M. M., *Christ and Horrors: The Coherence of Christology* (Cambridge: Cambridge University Press, 2006).

Basil, St, the Great, *On the Holy Spirit* (Crestwood, NY: St Vladimir's Seminary Press, 1980).

Calvin, J., *Hebrews and 1&2 Peter* (Grand Rapids, MI: Eerdmans, 1963).

Calvin, J., *Institutes of the Christian Religion* (Philadelphia, PA: Westminster Press, 1960).

Crisp, O., *Revisioning Christology: Theology in the Reformed Tradition* (Farnham: Ashgate, 2011).

Davies, J. A., *A Royal Priesthood: Literary and Intertextual Perspectives on an Image of Israel in Exodus 19.6* (London: T&T Clark International, 2004).

Driel, E. C. van, *Incarnation Anyway: Arguments for Supralapsarian Christology* (Oxford: Oxford University Press, 2008).

Farrow, D., *Ascension and Ecclesia: On the Significance of the Doctrine of the Ascension for Ecclesiology and Christian Cosmology* (Edinburgh: T&T Clark, 1999).

Farrow, D., *Ascension Theology* (London: T&T Clark International, 2011).

Gunton, C., *Christ and Creation* (Eugene, OR: Wipf and Stock, 1992).

Koester, C. R., *Hebrews: A New Translation, with Introduction and Commentary* (New Haven, CT: Yale University Press, 2001).

Moffitt, D., '"If Another Priest Arises": Jesus' Resurrection and the High Priestly Christology of Hebrews', in *A Cloud of Witnesses: The Theology of Hebrews in its Ancient Contexts*, ed. R. Bauckham, T. Hart, N. McDonald and D. Driver (London: T&T Clark, 2008), pp. 68–79.

O'Collins, G. and M. K. Jones, *Jesus our Priest: A Christian Approach to the Priesthood of Christ* (Oxford: Oxford University Press, 2010).

Pannenberg, W., *Jesus – God and Man* (London: SCM Press, 1968).

Tomlin, G., *The Prodigal Spirit: The Trinity, the Church and the Future of the World* (London: Alpha International, 2011).

Torrance, J., *Worship, Community, and the Triune God of Grace* (Carlisle: Paternoster Press, 1996).

3 Priesthood questioned

Billings, J. T., *Calvin, Participation and the Gift: The Activity of Believers in Union with Christ* (Oxford: Oxford University Press, 2007).

Brunner, E., *The Mediator: A Study of the Central Doctrine of the Christian Faith* (London: Lutterworth Press, 1934).

Calvin, J., *Calvin: Theological Treatises*, ed. and trans. J. K. S. Reid (Philadelphia, PA: Westminster Press, 1954).

Calvin, J., *Institutes of the Christian Religion* (Philadelphia, PA: Westminster Press, 1960).

Canlis, J., *Calvin's Ladder: A Spiritual Theology of Ascent and Ascension* (Grand Rapids, MI: Eerdmans, 2010).

Chrysostom, St John, *Six Books on the Priesthood* (Crestwood, NY: St Vladimir's Seminary Press, 1984).

Gerrish, B. A., 'Priesthood and Ministry: Luther's Fifth Means of Grace', in *The Old Protestantism and the New: Essays on the Reformation Heritage* (Edinburgh: T&T Clark, 1982), pp. 90–105.

Goergen, D. J. and A. Garrido, eds, *The Theology of Priesthood* (Collegeville, MN: Michael Glazier, 2000).

Lazareth, W. H., *Christians in Society: Luther, the Bible, and Social Ethics* (Minneapolis, MN: Fortress, 2001).

Luther, M., *Luther's Works*, ed. J. Pelikan et al., 55 vols (St Louis, MO: Concordia Publishing House, 1955–).

O'Collins, G. and M. K. Jones, *Jesus our Priest: A Christian Approach to the Priesthood of Christ* (Oxford: Oxford University Press, 2010).

Swanson, R. N., *Religion and Devotion in Europe c.1215–c.1515* (Cambridge: Cambridge University Press, 1995).

Tomlin, G., *The Prodigal Spirit: The Trinity, the Church and the Future of the World* (London: Alpha International, 2011).

Wengert, T. J., *Priesthood, Pastors, Bishops: Public Ministry for the Reformation and Today* (Minneapolis, MN: Fortress Press, 2008).

4 The priesthood of humanity

Basil, St, the Great, *On the Human Condition* (Crestwood, NY: St Vladimir's Seminary Press, 2005).

Bauckham, R., *The Bible and Ecology* (London: DLT, 2010).

Bauckham, R., *God and the Crisis of Freedom: Biblical and Contemporary Perspectives* (Louisville, KY: Westminster John Knox Press, 2002).

Bauckham, R., 'Modern Domination of Nature: Historical Origins and Biblical Critique', in *Environmental Stewardship* ed. R. J. Berry (London: T&T Clark, 2006), pp. 32–50.

Begbie, J., *Voicing Creation's Praise: Towards a Theology of the Arts* (London: T&T Clark, 1991).

Calvin, J., *Institutes of the Christian Religion* (Philadelphia, PA: Westminster Press, 1960).

Charry, E. T., *God and the Art of Happiness* (Grand Rapids, MI: Eerdmans, 2010).

Gunton, C., *Christ and Creation* (Eugene, OR: Wipf and Stock, 1992).

Moltmann, J., *God in Creation: An Ecological Doctrine of Creation* (London: SCM Press, 1985).

Theokritoff, E., 'Creation and Priesthood in Modern Orthodox Thinking', *Ecotheology* 10.3 (2005), 344–63.

Torrance, T. F., *Transformation and Convergence in the Frame of Knowledge. Explorations in the Interrelations of Scientific and Theological Enterprise* (Belfast: Christian Journals, 1984).

White, L., 'The Historical Roots of our Ecological Crisis', *Science* 155 (1967), 1203–7.

Zizioulas, J., 'Priest of Creation', *Environmental Stewardship: Critical Perspectives – Past and Present*, ed. R. J. Berry (London: T&T Clark, 2006), pp. 273–90.

5 The priesthood of the Church

Barth, K., *Church Dogmatics* (London: T&T Clark, 2009).

Basil, St, the Great, *On the Holy Spirit* (Crestwood, NY: St Vladimir's Seminary Press, 1980).

Jinkins, M., *The Church Faces Death: Ecclesiology in a Post-Modern Context* (Oxford: Oxford University Press, 1999).

McDonald, S., *Re-Imaging Election: Divine Election as Representing God to Others and Others to God* (Grand Rapids, MI: Eerdmans, 2010).

Robinson, J. A. T., *On Being the Church in the World* (London: SCM Press, 1960).

Seitz, C. R., *Figured Out: Typology and Providence in Christian Scripture* (Louisville, KY: Westminster John Knox Press, 2001).

Sheils, W. J., ed., *The Church and Healing*, Studies in Church History (Oxford: Basil Blackwell, 1982).

Torrance, J., *Worship, Community, and the Triune God of Grace* (Carlisle: Paternoster Press, 1996).

6 The priesthood of ministers

Allen, R., *Missionary Methods: St Paul's or Ours?* (Grand Rapids, MI: Eerdmans, 1983).

Baptism, Eucharist and Ministry (Geneva: World Council of Churches, 1982).

Barth, K., *Church Dogmatics* (London: T&T Clark, 2009).

Calvin, J., *Institutes of the Christian Religion* (Philadelphia, PA: Westminster Press, 1960).

Chrysostom, St John, *Six Books on the Priesthood* (Crestwood, NY: St Vladimir's Press, 1984).

Greenwood, R., *Transforming Priesthood: A New Theology of Mission and Ministry* (London: SPCK, 1994).

Handy, C., *The Empty Raincoat: Making Sense of the Future* (London: Arrow, 1995).

Hanson, A., *Church Sacraments and Ministry* (London: Mowbray, 1975).

Harmless, W., *Augustine and the Catechumenate* (Collegeville, MN: Liturgical Press, 1995).

Milner, B. C., *Calvin's Doctrine of the Church* (Leiden: Brill, 1970).

Moberly, R. C., *Ministerial Priesthood* (London: SPCK, 1969).

Moltmann, J., *A Broad Place: An Autobiography* (London: SCM Press, 2007).

Newbigin, L., *The Household of God* (London: SCM Press, 1957).

Tomlin, G., *The Provocative Church* (London: SPCK, 2014).

Volf, M., *After Our Likeness: The Church as the Image of the Trinity* (Grand Rapids, MI: Eerdmans, 1998).

7 Priestly leadership

Chrysostom, St John, *Six Books on the Priesthood* (Crestwood, NY: St Vladimir's Seminary Press, 1984).

Fedwick, P. J., *The Church and the Charisma of Leadership in Basil of Caesarea* (Toronto: Pontifical Institute of Mediaeval Studies, 1979).

Francis, Pope, *Apostolic Exhortation: Evangelii Gaudium* (Vatican City: Vatican Press, 2014).

Hock, R. F., 'Paul's Tentmaking and the Problem of his Social Class', *JBL* 97 (1978), 555–64.

Hock, R. F., *The Social Context of Paul's Ministry: Tentmaking and Apostleship* (Philadelphia, PA: Fortress Press, 1980).

Horsley, R., ed., *Paul and Empire: Religion and Power in Roman Imperial Society* (Harrisburg, PA: Trinity Press International, 1997).

Lewis-Anthony, J., *If You Meet George Herbert on the Road, Kill Him: Radically Re-thinking Priestly Ministry* (London: Continuum, 2009).

Lewis-Anthony, J., *You are the Messiah, and I Should Know: Why Leadership is a Myth (and Probably a Heresy)* (London: Bloomsbury, 2013).

Pannenberg, W., *Jesus – God and Man* (London: SCM Press, 1968).

Epilogue

Kidner, D., *Psalms 1–72: An Introduction and Commentary* (Nottingham: Inter-Varsity Press, 1978; repr. 2008).

Tate, M. E., *Psalms 51–150* (Nashville, TN: Thomas Nelson, 2010).

Weiser, A., *The Psalms: A Commentary*, trans. Herbert Hartwell (London: SCM Press, 1962).

Did you know that SPCK is a registered charity?

As well as publishing great books by leading Christian authors, we also . . .

. . . **make assemblies meaningful and fun for over a million children** by running www.assemblies.org.uk, a popular website that provides free assembly scripts for teachers. For many children, school assembly is the only contact they have with Christian faith and culture, and the only time in their week for spiritual reflection.

. . . **help prisoners become confident readers** with our easy-to-read stories. Poor literacy is a huge barrier to rehabilitation. Prisoners identify with the believable heroes of our gritty fiction, but questions at the end of each chapter help them to examine their choices from a moral perspective and to build their reading confidence.

. . . **support student ministers overseas in their training.** We give them free, specially written theology books, the International Study Guides. These books really do make a difference, not just to students but to ministers and, through them, to a whole community.

Please support these great schemes: visit www.spck.org.uk/support-us to find out more.